THE
FOLSOM PRISON
BLOODY 13

THE
FOLSOM PRISON
BLOODY 13

The Big Escape of 1903

JOSH MORGAN

THE
History
PRESS

Published by The History Press
Charleston, SC
www.historypress.com

First published 2024

Manufactured in the United States

ISBN 9781467155939

Library of Congress Control Number: 2023950814

Notice: The information in this book is true and complete to the best of our knowledge. It is offered without guarantee on the part of the author or The History Press. The author and The History Press disclaim all liability in connection with the use of this book.

This book is dedicated to my wife, Sheri, who provided me with support and encouragement, and my mother, Lynne, who instilled in me an awareness and love of our family story and how it is part of California's history.

Main Gate, 1902. *Courtesy of Folsom Historical Society.*

CONTENTS

ACKNOWLEDGEMENTS

The telling of this story started as a discussion around the table during a Sunday dinner with extended family. I was talking about a letter that seemed to have a good story and how we couldn't figure out what it was referencing and also had trouble reading the text. My mother-in-law, Barbara, offered to read the letter and others we had from the same era and transcribe them.

Once I found the beginnings of a story that had not been widely told, I reached out far and wide and am grateful to the incredibly dedicated staffs and volunteers at the California State Archives; the Sacramento Room of the Sacramento County Public Library; the El Dorado County Historical Museum; the Folsom History Museum; the San Joaquin County Historical Museum; the Contra Costa Historical Society; April Moore, who wrote about the executions at Folsom Prison, William Berg, who writes extensively about the history of Sacramento; and Jim Brown and Duke Juanitas from the Folsom Prison Museum.

Once the story was coming together, I am grateful to Annette Kassis and Rodi Lee, who provided professional perspective as early readers to this first-time writer, and Laurie Krill and The History Press, who believed in this story and helped bring it to print.

INTRODUCTION

Many people's introduction to Folsom Prison is the iconic lyrics by Johnny Cash, where he sings about his despair of being stuck at Folsom Prison while life outside keeps moving on without him. In Northern California most are aware the song has little accuracy from a geographic standpoint—don't get me started on why he's in a California State Prison if he "shot a man in Reno [Nevada]"—but there is accuracy in not seeing the sunshine and that time keeps dragging on. While Johnny Cash was never a prisoner at Folsom, he did perform a concert for prisoners there in 1968.

Sixty-five years before Cash played his iconic concert, Folsom Prison was already notorious as one of the most feared prisons in the country. Inmates were kept in dark cells with solid rock walls and often tied up for days at a time in straitjackets as punishment. One warden who came to Folsom arrived after a tumultuous tenure at California's first state prison at San Quentin.

While the cells had thick walls made of stone quarried from the surrounding hillsides, the prison itself didn't have encircling walls until 1907, nearly thirty years after opening. There were some gates and fenced-off sections, but the jailers relied on the natural barriers created by the American River and the surrounding hills, as funding to complete the curtain walls hadn't been approved, perhaps due to the strong forces focused on making money off prisoners at San Quentin who wanted to see Folsom fail.

The tasks were increased, the food rations cut, and even the convict stripes were made thinner and cheaper. These abuses, coupled with brutal straitjacketings for the slightest infraction of rules, crystallized all the hatred, despair, and hopelessness in the prison. All the convicts needed was an organizer, a leader. He appeared in the person of Dick Gordon. With a sentence of forty-five years and a prior prison experience, Gordon saw no chance of getting out on the square and began planning to escape. He was young—about twenty-three—modest, kindly, intelligent.[1]

This was not a time of reform for prisoners; the focus was punishment, and Folsom excelled at punishment. This worked until it didn't, when prisoners rebelled, attacked their jailors and made breaks for freedom. These attempts usually ended quickly and bloodily for both the prisoners and the guards, but there was one time when some got away. This is the story of that time.

Etta Steinman was twenty-two years old in 1903. Like many in this era, she had a spirited correspondence with quite a few people with letters back and forth filled with gossip, well wishes and stories of travels. One letter stands out: it tells the story of how the author, whom we believe to be Albert Wilkinson, the son of the warden of Folsom Prison and one of Etta's close friends, was awakened early in the morning of July 27, 1903, and told that his father along with several others had been taken captive by escaped prisoners and were being "cut to pieces." Like many first reports of violence, there's an element of truth in that statement, along with more of a story. There were indeed men who lost their lives that day and others whose lives changed forever.

Etta was my great-grandmother, and while our lives overlapped only by a few years, her presence and that of her father continue to be a part of my life. She grew up in Sacramento at the turn of the twentieth century, at a time when the world was switching from horses to cars and fire and gas to electricity. She had a front-row seat for both, as her father, my great-great grandfather B.U. Steinman, was the mayor of Sacramento in the 1890s and, among other business interests, the president of the Sacramento Gas and Electric Company, which ran power lines from a dam at Folsom to power Sacramento twenty-three miles away.

There are themes in this story that ring true today, with some convicts' actions driven by addiction to drugs, allegations of brutality to inmates, systemic racism and conflicting reports in the media. Contemporary media reports were often written with second- or thirdhand or, in some cases, seemingly made-up information and were many times contradictory. This narrative tries to paint a cohesive picture of what happened that summer in the Northern California Gold Country and why. Anything in quotes is from a contemporaneous source; however, as you'll see, some of the language seems contrived and was likely created by overenthusiastic reporters of the time.

More than one hundred years later, we still don't know the whole story, but from what we know of the events surrounding July 27, 1903, it included corrupt management, cruel punishment and poor design, which led to a story of brutality, escape, heroism and mysteries that still hasn't ended.

THE PEOPLE OF THE FOLSOM PRISON BREAK OF 1903

List of Convicts Who Escaped Folsom Prison on July 27, 1903, and the Crimes for Which They Were Originally Sentenced

John Joseph "J.J." "The Lone Kid" Allison, four years, robbery and burglary/
    second degree
Frank Case, life, robbery
Edward Davis, thirty-three years, robbery
Harry "The Borer" Eldridge, thirty years, robbery
Ray Fahey, life, robbery
Richard M. "Red" Gordon, forty-five years, robbery
Fred Howard, fifteen years, robbery
Frank "The Little Dutchman" Miller, twelve years, burglary/first degree
Joseph Murphy, fourteen years, burglary
James P. "Smiley" Roberts, twenty years, robbery
Albert Seavis, twenty-five years, burglary
Joseph Theron, life, robbery
John H. "Tex" Wood, life, robbery

Folsom Prison Staff

Thomas Wilkinson, warden
Harry Wilkinson, stenographer (the warden's grandson)
R.J. Murphy, captain of the guard
W.A. Chalmers, gatekeeper
William Cotter, guard
Joseph Cochrane, general overseer
Guy Jeter, foreman of the prison quarry
Henry Kipp, lieutenant of the guard
J.G. McDonough, general overseer
Charles Ward, master mechanic
J. Klenzendorf, guard
L.C. Vetress Jr., guard
Guy Jeter, guard
Charles H. Jolly, guard
O. Seavy, guard
James Dolan, guard
William Hopton, guard
T.C. Brown, stagecoach driver
Archibald Yell, warden

Law

Placer County

Charles Keena, sheriff, Placer County
Lee Coan, deputy
Frank H. Depender, deputy

El Dorado County

Archie Bosquit, sheriff, El Dorado County (father of John Bosquit)
John Bosquit, deputy
Louis Phillip (Will) Stringer, civilian/volunteer

Sacramento County

Elijah Carson Hart, judge
David Reese, sheriff, Sacramento County
Edward Reese, deputy, Sacramento County (son of David Reese)
Brown, undersheriff
Griffin, deputy sheriff
Jack Hunter, deputy
George Winterbrock, deputy

Amador County

Tomas K. Norman, sheriff, Amador County

Reno, Nevada

John Hayes, sheriff, Washoe County
Sharkey, deputy
William Maxwell, deputy
Charles Leeper, chief of police, Reno, Nevada

Company H

Captain Charles Swisler
Lieutenant Smith
Festus Rutherford
Will Rutherford
A.J. Bell
Bill Burgess
Griffith Jones
Henry Walters
A.W. Gill
William Blake

Other Prisoners at Folsom Prison

Andy Myers
William A. Leverone
Joseph Casey, trusty
O.C. Clark, trusty
Charles Abbott
John Martinez

State of California

Governor George Pardee

Citizens

Elizabeth "Lizzie" Cosens, resident of El Dorado County (wife of George F.)
George F. Cosens, resident of El Dorado County (husband of Lizzie)
Sanford Diehl and family
Anna Jurgens
Andrew Kamenzind
Fred Twitchell
W.W. Hoyt, El Dorado County supervisor (Twitchell's grandfather)
David Gipe, caretaker of the Grand Victory Mine
Louis Meiss, rancher in El Dorado County

SEPTEMBER 16, 1903

From the San Francisco Call

"RED SHIRT" GORDON NOW IN CUSTODY
Convict Is Captured—by an Officer in Texas.
Desperate Leader of Convicts Is Run Down in Lone Star State.
Special Dispatch to The Call.

A telegram was just received by Warden Wilkinson from W.B. Mathis, an officer in Jacksonville, Tex., conveying the information that he had in custody convict 474S, Richard M. Gordon, one of the men who escaped in the jail break of July 27, and asking the amount of the reward. There can be no question but that the Texas officer has the right man, but how he was captured is a mystery. as there are no particulars at hand.

"Red Shirt" Gordon was considered to be the shrewdest and most desperate of the fugitive convicts and the authorities had but very little hope of ever recapturing him. After the convicts had succeeded in their break and had got beyond the prison grounds. Gordon, realizing that he would stand a better chance of escaping: if alone, suddenly dropped away from the crowd and was not missed for quite a while. The other convicts were very much incensed at Gordon for his doing as he did and swore vengeance on him if any of them ever chanced to meet him. His presence in Texas shows the man's resourcefulness in getting far away from the scene of the prison break and the subsequent man hunt.[2]

Officer Mathis's telegram would have put an end to the saga of one of the biggest prison breaks in United States history if Gordon had been subsequently returned to California, but he wasn't. He was then also reported dead in Missouri several years later, but he was never returned to California.

EARLY CALIFORNIA

You are without a single police officer or watchman, and have not the means of confining a prisoner for an hour; neither have you a place to shelter, while living, sick and unfortunate strangers who may be cast upon our shores, or to bury them when dead.
—John W. Geary, last alcalde and first mayor of San Francisco, 1849

January 24, 1848

The Sierra Nevada rise from the valley floor in California and run four hundred miles along the eastern edge of California. The foothills of El Dorado County rise to the mountains and include an area along the South Fork American River, which flows through Coloma.

James Marshall was thirty-four when he made the decision to come west in 1844 after a youth spent in Hope Township, Hunterdon County, New Jersey, where his father had apprenticed him to a wainwright (wagon builder). This opportunity for a career wasn't enough to stop his wanderlust and desire to see the West. He started west and first went to Crawfordsville, Indiana, then Warsaw, Illinois, and then nearly to Fort Leavenworth, Missouri. Each time, Marshall stayed just long enough to learn that wasn't where he wanted to be.

He eventually determined California was the West he had to be looking for and joined a wagon train of nearly one hundred wagons heading for the territory. His part of the group entered California in the far north of the territory near Mount Shasta, a fourteen-thousand-plus-foot elevation semidormant volcano, and he made his way south to Sacramento, where he eventually went to work for area pioneer John Sutter, with one of his jobs being to help build a lumber mill in the foothills east of the settlement.

> *Coloma, first named "Culloomah," was situated in a little valley along the South Fork of the American River, in what is now a portion of El Dorado County. The hills north of the river were very rugged and precipitous, but on the south side the declivity was more gradual, and here on a point of landforms by a curve in the stream, Marshall found an ideal location for the building. The water power was ample and the surrounding hills were covered with timber.*[3]

Marshall hired Peter Wimmer and a crew of hands, including James Bargee, Henry Bigler, Jas. Brown, William Johnson, William Scott and Alexander Stephens, to help build the mill.[4] Along with this group were "eight or ten Indians, who were employed at the time in throwing out the larger stones excavated while the millrace was being constructed during the day. At night, the gate of the fore-bay being raised, the water entered and carried away the sand, gravel, and the smaller stones."

It was in the millrace of the sawmill where on January 24, 1848, James Marshall's eye was caught by something shiny. He walked the millrace each morning, as he had suspicions there may be valuable minerals being washed down the riverbed, and until this morning he hadn't found anything other than rocks and sand. Then, just under the water, there was something on the granite. He picked it up, and it might have been mica but seemed too heavy. So maybe it was copper or even gold. Gold is malleable, and copper is brittle. If a yellowish rock bends or dents under pressure, it might be gold; if it breaks, it might be copper.

Marshall set the small piece he'd found on a flat nearby rock and picked up another rock in his hand. He struck down, and when he hit the nugget he'd found, for a nugget it was, it dented and didn't break. Over the next few days, he picked up several more pieces and collected gold dust. When he had enough to be sure of what was in the area, he decided to head back down the hill to Sacramento and let his boss, John Sutter, know what he'd found. Along the way, he kept an eye on the river, looking for suitable areas to float lumber down from the mill, which he'd been hired to do, and also for more of the gold.

This started the California gold rush, which over the next few years brought tens of thousands of fortune seekers to California.

Mining progressed from picking nuggets out of stream beds to hydraulic mining, where jets of water were blasted at cliffs to uncover the gold underneath, to pit mining, where ore was quarried out through manual labor and dynamite and then processed in stamp mills that crushed the rock to extract the gold.

3

LOCKED UP IN THE LAND OF GOLD

Convicts are to be respectful and obedient to the officers;
industrious and submissive to the rules and regulations of the Prison;
to obey all orders promptly.
—"Rules for Convicts at the State-Prison,"
California Board of Prison Directors, May 5, 1858

OCTOBER 8, 1849

California as a civil society followed California as a place, an idea and a reality. As California grew from approximately 10,000 non-Native people in 1848, to more than 92,000 in 1850 when it became a state and then to almost 380,000 in 1860, the need for infrastructure followed.

Incarceration in California began as a series of prison ships during the gold rush, following a speech by the first alcalde of the District of San Francisco, Colonel John W. Geary, who said, "You are without a single police officer or watchman, and have not the means of confining a prisoner for an hour; neither have you a place to shelter, while living, sick and unfortunate strangers who may be cast upon our shores, or to bury them when dead."[5]

This call for a municipal infrastructure led to public funds being allocated for various improvements, and the first priority was for a prison, with the current facilities used as jails being deemed wholly inadequate.

"The first money appropriated by the ayuntamiento [town council] was for the purchase of the brig Euphemia, which was converted into a prison for the confinement of criminals. This was the first jail established in the place where convicted rogues could be kept in custody."[6]

ACCORDING TO LEGEND, EUPHEMIA was persecuted for her Christian faith in AD 303 and, perhaps foreshadowing her role in California, was executed by bear attack in an arena in Chalcedon near present-day Istanbul, Turkey.

On October 8, 1849, *Euphemia* was purchased from a member of the ayuntamiento named William Heath Davis for $3,500,[7] setting a precedent for some penal decisions in California to be based on who they benefited rather than for the public good. The ship was purchased as a stranded hulk and converted to a jail with another roughly $1,000 worth of lumber and then fitted out with $500 worth of balls and chains.

Following a pattern still often followed in penal systems, the *Euphemia* was for housing not only criminals but also the mentally ill. "The Euphemia continued to serve as a retention facility for the criminal and the insane until 1851; thereafter the mentally ill were confined in station houses, which were to become the first asylums. The records show that inmates who were insane numbered 14 in 1850, 22 in 1851, 34 in 1852, and 65 in 1853."[8]

Like many things in a boomtown economy, the *Euphemia* was something repurposed and used until it was forgotten. As tens of thousands of gold seekers arrived in San Francisco Bay to find their fortune, the ships that brought them were often abandoned, and by 1850, it was estimated there were more than seven hundred ships left with no crew and no means to move them. Ships were converted to lodging houses, offices and warehouses, with the most famous being the *Niantic*,[9] which was purchased and pulled into the flats of San Francisco, where it became a warehouse. As San Francisco grew, land was filled in, and the city grew around and then finally over the *Niantic*, until it burned in one of the many fires that destroyed much of the city that would come to signify itself with a phoenix. A building was built above it, and it was forgotten until 1978, when it was unearthed while excavating for the Mark Twain Plaza next to the iconic Transamerica Pyramid and was now six blocks from the waterfront given the continued filling in of the bay wetlands to reclaim ever more land for the insatiable growth of California. It was an exciting twist of fate that it was one of the most well-known chroniclers of the gold rush and early California who was indirectly responsible for this discovery.

The *Niantic* wasn't the only former ship to end up a permanent part of the San Francisco landscape. After the *Euphemia* was abandoned and burned to the waterline, it, too, became part of the fill that today is rumored to be below the intersection of Battery and Sacramento Streets.

JULY 14, 1852

San Quentin opened on July 14, 1852, as the first state prison in California. Set on twenty acres on a peninsula in Marin County, it jutted into the bay across from San Francisco, where inmates could see one of the fastest-growing cities in the world but were a world apart. While the location on the edge of San Francisco Bay may sound luxurious, it was cold, wet, buffeted by strong winds coming in through the Golden Gate and muffled in fog that blanketed the bay and made dark cells even darker.

July 14, 1852, is given as the opening of San Quentin; this was likely the date the *Waban*, a bark that had arrived in San Francisco Bay in 1850 bearing hopeful argonauts, was towed to the location near the coast of Marin. A bark, or barque, was a three-masted ship designed with rigging that allowed the vessel to be operated by smaller crews than were required for traditional full-rigged ships, which made them the perfect workhorses of the age of sail. The *Waban* wasn't necessarily a large ship, displacing 268 tons (compared to 46,329 tons displaced by the *Titanic* seventy years later).

The *Waban* had followed *Euphemia* as a prison ship on San Francisco Bay.

Prisoner ships such as the Euphemia and the Waban were typically crowded with prisoners living in undesirable conditions. The ships generally included officer and guard quarters as well as a kitchen, a dining hall for convicts, and a cell facility. Prison inspection records for the Waban detailed the prison ship's conditions. According to the prison records, 150 men confined at night in quarters designed for a maximum of 50 individuals resulted in air so foul that the convicts' health suffered; moreover, the facility lacked a hospital to care for the sick. Prisoner escapes were prevalent also, likely because of a lack of distinguishable prisoner uniforms and the open nature of the prisoners' work (during the day, the inmates worked in an open, unsecured space).[10]

On December 18, 1851,[11] the first inmates were locked in makeshift cells, as the ship that had come to California filled with men full of dreams now locked up those who had to be removed from society. At night on the *Waban*, four men were locked in each eight-by-eight-foot space. The conditions were so crowded and dangerous that guards wouldn't spend the night, and once prisoners were locked in, the staff left until morning. When the guards arrived in the morning, any prisoners who had died during the night were removed and buried on shore. There usually weren't any questions asked.[12]

The first cell block, which began construction in 1853, was referred to as "The Stones." It had forty-eight cells with thick doors and no windows and was designed to house 250 inmates, but this was quickly exceeded as California's free and incarcerated population grew rapidly. Overcrowding led to substandard conditions where violence and disease ran rampant. Like many prisons at the time, San Quentin was privately managed, and the prison operators hired out inmates for work to generate profits. The lack of attention paid to the care of inmates caught the attention of many, including the *San Francisco Daily Bulletin*, which wrote of the builder of San Quentin, J.M. Estell, "having wrung from the Treasury money enough to erect a palace of marble, [Estell] has built a miserable, tumble-down half-burned-brick house, in which the prisoners are herded together in long apartments, without distinction of age, or offense like wild cattle in a corral."[13] Estell was also said to have at one time denied food service to the entire prison for a solid week and created an atmosphere of abuse by guards in which female prisoners were sexually assaulted.[14]

Questions and concerns about San Quentin were nothing new, as controversy and grift had been part of the peninsula where the prison was built since its original land grant in 1840. The recipient of the grant, Juan B. Cooper, sold the entire allotment of 4,400 acres for $32,500 to Benjamin Buckelew in 1850. Buckelew then turned around and, in 1852, after a sustained campaign to impress state prison officials, sold twenty acres for $10,000, despite public comment at the time that the land was worth no more than $5 per acre.

MAY 5, 1858

Just seven years after the arrival of the first inmates, there were serious concerns about San Quentin.

On May 5, 1858, California's Board of Prison Directors formally adopted recommendations from state executives including the governor, lieutenant governor and secretary of state for attempting to moderate growing concerns with prisoner behavior. The "recommendations" were the "Rules for Convicts at the State-Prison," which at that time was San Quentin.

The rules read:

> *Convicts are to be respectful and obedient to the officers; industrious and submissive to the rules and regulations of the Prison; to obey all orders promptly. When about to speak to an officer; to salute him, by raising the hand to the forehead. To exhibit an ill-temper when reproved or admonished by an officer; nor to have unnecessary conversation or enter into any collusive proceedings with an officer; or have unnecessary conversation with convicts or unto them; nor speak to any person from without the prison; nor answer any questions from such a one but by permission of the Warden. Not to look at visitors. Nor leave the stand for labor; nor go out of the place of labor without permission of an officer. They are not permitted to have any snuff or tobacco; nor to have pens, pencils, ink, or paper, without permission. Nor to carry food into the yard or shops; nor to make any alteration whatever in their clothing, with permission of the officer.*
>
> *They are to be prompt in taking their proper place in the division at bellringing. To march in close order, body erect, and hands by the side of the thighs, and occupy such seats as may be assigned them.*
>
> *They are to be cleanly in person, clothing, and cell. To use the spit-dish when necessary, and not spit on or out of the door, nor on the walls or floor. They are not to mark, scratch, or in any way mar or disfigure the cell, nor push open the door with the feet. Not to injure or misuse any book, dish, or other article or thing whatever, allowed in the cell. Not to make any change, by bringing in or carrying out any article from the cell, contrary to regulation. Bed and bedding, to be kept in good order. Not to rap on the doors except in case of sickness, or of absolute necessity.*

At the ringing of the first bell in the morning, they are to turn out, dress, fasten up the cot, and have the bucket ready for marching out. At the order, they are to throw the door open gently, to the wall, step out, and march, when ordered.

In marching into the room where divine service is to be performed, each convict is to take the seat assigned him, and while there to give his entire attention to the services. All disposition to cough, as far as possible to be suppressed; and no shuffling with the feet; or movement of the body, calculated to disturb the order and quiet of the service, be indulged in or practiced.

If unwell, and needing the advice of the Physician, they are to report to the officer of their department, immediately after marching in, in the morning. If sent to the Hospital, they must proceed directly to that place, and await the decision of the Physician. When ordered to the yard, for exercise and air, they must confine themselves within the limits of that part of the yard designated for that purpose.

When wishing to speak with the Warden, or to have an interview with any other officer, the convict is to make known his desire to his officer, and in no case to speak to either in any place without permission of said officer.

We are directed by the Governor to say that the record of punishments, which the Warden is required to keep, will be closely examined in all cases where applications for pardon or restoration to citizenship are made, and no one whose conduct has been bad, can expect any clemency from him.

John B. Weller }
Joseph Walkup } State-Prison Directors
Ferris Forman }[15]

The rules reflected a martial attitude that included saluting officers, marching in formation and requesting permission to speak. With a focus on submission and punishment, there is no mention of any restorative or rehabilitative practices.

The growth in population of California and San Quentin quickly led the state government to pass legislation in 1858 titled "An Act for the Government of the State Prison Conflicts, and to Provide for the Location of a Branch Prison," supporting a new state prison to be built at a site that had not been determined. There were three frontrunners for the location, all near the state capital of Sacramento.

Folsom was ultimately chosen as the location partly because of the opportunities provided by the site, with the American River providing a border and natural barrier and potential power source and the hills offering seemingly inexhaustible supplies of granite to be quarried, shaped and broken down as well as for use in building the prison itself.

Penal and incarceration theory in the United States at the time focused on two methods, with the most prevalent being the Auburn or congregant system, named after the prison in Auburn, New York, which focused on inmates working together in groups during the day and being locked up individually or in smaller groups at night. The alternative was the Pennsylvania or separate system, which completely isolated inmates from one another to the point that arriving inmates were hooded so they could not see and then blocked from any contact with other inmates during the extent of their stay.

Both methods had a theoretical goal of rehabilitation, with it being driven by hard work in the Auburn model and solitude in the Pennsylvania, but led to opportunities for abuse of prisoners by overseers. While each had its own opportunities for abuse, both extensively used restraints of many kinds as punishment.

At Eastern State Penitentiary, which championed the Pennsylvania model, one of the punishments was the "mad chair," which looked like a barber chair. Prisoners were strapped so tightly their circulation would be cut off. For some prisoners, this led to amputation of limbs, and others to insanity. At Folsom, the method of restraint was often "the jacket," also known as Susie's Corset or the Bag, which former inmate Jack Black described as:

> heavy canvas about four feet long and wide enough to go around a man's body. There were long pockets sewed to the inner side of it into which my arms were thrust. I was then thrown to the floor face down and the jacket was laced up the back. The edges of the jacket were fitted with eyeholes and the thing was tightened up with a soft, stout rope just as a lady's shoe is laced. It can be drawn tight enough to stop the circulation of blood or breath.[16]

An even more graphic description was given in a report to the California Assembly in 1911, when it was investigating the use of cruel and unusual punishments in California prisons:

The straitjacket. This punishment consists of placing the convict in a jacket made of heavy, strong, canvas, cut so as to fit the body and shoulders of the wearer, along the edges of which there is a row of strong eyelets. The jacket extends from the throat down to and below the knees. On the inside there are two loops, or places where the hands of the wearer are placed, so that the hands rest upon and in front of the upper portion of the legs. The jacket is placed upon the convict, he is then laid down upon his face, and the jacket, by means of a quarter. inch rope through the eyelets on the edge thereof, is laced upon the body.

The jacket by these means may be laced up tight enough to inflict great physical pain, and even death, by impeding breathing, and pressure on the heart and kidneys The convict is kept in the jacket such a length of time as is necessary in the discretion of the warden, in no case exceeding six hours, consecutively, in any one day.

Other punishments in use at the time at both Folsom and San Quentin were solitary confinement, solitary confinement on bread and water, cuffing up, "standing between doors" and "tricing up." Prisoners who were punished by standing between doors were forced to stand in the doorway of their cell with a rack or a grate behind them and the door in front of them. They would then remain there for up to eighteen out of twenty-four hours, starting at 6:00 a.m., then removed at noon, put back between doors at 1:00 p.m., removed at 7:00 p.m. and finally put back at 9:00 p.m. until 2:00 am.

While standing was certainly tedious, it may not have been as painful as "tricing up," where the arms of the inmate were handcuffed behind them and then secured to a hook in the wall and cinched up until their wrists were behind their neck. They would be left in this position for up an hour and fifteen minutes at a time and four times per day, leading to up to five hours of torture out of twenty-four.

In the early days of San Quentin, punishment also went beyond aggressive restraint into institutionally sanctioned assaults and beatings. In the 1850s, George W. Wells served as captain of the guard and had a "duty" to beat inmates.

"I have the (duty of) inflicting all punishment," said Captain Wells. "I use a rawhide or leather strap. Any violation of Prison discipline, such as attempts to escape, insurrections, stealing, using offensive language, fighting, unnecessary noise, disorderly or vicious conduct, render them liable. (Lashes were given) ranging from five up. No other person employed in the Prison is permitted to inflict any punishment, except during my absence, when I deputize someone. But the business is generally laid over until my return."[17]

California went with the Auburn Model.

With the adoption of the Auburn Model, there was a need for industry. One of the reasons Folsom was selected as the location for the new prison was proximity to the American River, which while serving as the northern border of the prison could also be tamed to provide power if the convicts built a canal and dam with a powerhouse for their use. The Natoma Water Company contracted for their labor for fifty cents per inmate per day paid to the prison, not the inmates, seemingly in conflict with then recent prohibitions on the hiring out of inmates. The first constructed buildings at the prison were built by a hired contractor for the first wave of prisoners to occupy.

"By general consent, one of the major requisites for a potential prison was the presence of material which would ensure labor for the inmates. Hard physical labor was a part of the concept of punishment in vogue in 19th century United States."[18]

Along with digging canals, at the site was a granite quarry that was described as having an inexhaustible supply of stone. However, it was seemingly exhausted by around 1904. The prison was also expected to be semi-self-sufficient and had shops that made ice, tinware, clothes, furniture, boots, bedding and a significant amount of the food consumed by inmates. This in-house industry required the use of many tools, including shovels, picks and files.

The tools that made the work possible could also be used for other purposes.

July 26, 1880

In late July, Folsom, California, has an average high temperature of ninety-four degrees Fahrenheit, and many days reach well over one hundred with little breeze to break up the heat. While there's low humidity, the extremely long days of sunshine, with sunrise before 6:00 a.m. and sunset after 8:00 p.m., keep the temperature from falling much overnight. This is a big difference from San Quentin, which is on the shore of a peninsula in Marin County, on the edge of San Francisco Bay and within sight of the

Cell blocks. *Courtesy of Folsom Historical Society.*

Golden Gate, which then was open with no bridge connecting Marin to San Francisco.

It was a hot, still day when the first forty-five inmates[19] arrived at Folsom Prison on July 26, 1880, likely angry and irritable after several hours on a hot train. They had been selected from the population at San Quentin. Some said they were among the toughest there and San Quentin leadership had sent them out of spite, as they viewed Folsom as cutting into their revenue from hiring out inmates for labor.

Inmate number 1 was assigned to Chong Hing of Canton, China,[20] who was serving time for arson, and the number selected for him may have been a play on racist stereotypes at the time that referred to Chinese men as "number one boy."[21] Hing, like the other inmates, was transferred from San Quentin by boat across San Francisco Bay to San Francisco and then to Oakland, where they were transferred to the Overland Express train for delivery to Folsom.

The first inmates were quickly joined by 50 more in mid-August, then 114 through mid-September. There were more than 200 inmates at Folsom by the end of the second month.

There were just over 100 miles separating San Quentin from Folsom, but the differences are vast. The first inmates were greeted by a long building nearly 500 feet up each side and almost a quarter mile around the perimeter. There were 328 cells, each "8 feet six inches by 7 feet one inch, the outer wall alone being pierced, and this closed by a heavy iron door two feet one inch by seven feet two inches. Each door had at the bottom six 1½ inch holes, and near the top a slot eight inches long. The door was secured by three broad, heavy strap-hinges, riveted clear across, and by two heavy two-inch iron bolts, with massive hasps clasping a common staple and secured by a great padlock."[22]

The cells were in two cell blocks with 166 cells in A-Block and 162 in B-Block. The cell blocks were each two stories high with iron in between the levels serving as the floor of the top level and ceiling of the bottom.

Most of the cells were designed to hold two inmates in their fifty-six square feet and had two wooden bunks with straw-filled bedding along with two buckets, one for water and one for waste, as there were no indoor toilets and prisoners would not be let out of their cells when nature called. Each morning when inmates were awakened at 6:00 a.m., they would line up outside their cells with their waste buckets in hand. The contents of the buckets would then be dumped into an opening in the floor that were opened by a set of hinged doors. Crushed limestone would then cover the waste, which would be flushed out of the trench by large buckets of water and flow down out of the building to the river. Inmates would then take their buckets back to their respective cells. The buckets were iron and, given their heft, in addition to being waste receptacles were sometimes used as weapons.

The walls of the main building were two and a half feet thick at ground level and built of large blocks of granite quarried on the site and resting on a foundation that went down seventeen feet and was eight feet thick. The ready supply of granite that was part of Folsom's selection was being put to good use.

The inmates also would have noticed what was missing from surrounding the prison—walls. There were no perimeter walls at Folsom Prison when it opened. The prison was on the east bank of the American River and on a flat plateau graded out from China Hill. The fast-moving water of the river ran ice-cold from snowmelt in the spring and warmed in the summer as it flowed down over dangerous rocks where it passed Folsom. The river and the clear-cut open hills with wide open fields of vision and fire for guards were seen as enough until first a stockade wall, then eventually a wall of granite, could be built.

In lieu of walls were chalk lines referred to as "deadman lines." These denoted a space where, if an inmate were over, any guard could make them a dead man. Between the guards walking the grounds with heavy lead-tipped canes and the guards in towers with rifles, manning Gatling guns, there were many ways for a prisoner to go from living to dead very quickly.

By the end of September 1880, there were more than two hundred prisoners, no walls and a lot of guns.

June 27, 1899

Thomas Wilkinson, the commissary at San Quentin Prison, was removed from his position at the action of the warden.

This may have been a surprise to Wilkinson and others, as he had recently been assured he would be able to remain in the position during a change in wardens. Incoming warden Aguirre was, like many at the time, able to make appointments as he wished, but in the meantime, he led "the board to believe that Thomas Wilkinson should remain as commissary. In fact, it is stated that the directors felt so positive of the retention of these two men that President Fitzgerald sent Wilkinson a telegram no later than last Tuesday telling him to be at his ease—everything had been fixed nicely." Then the directors later notified "Wilkinson that on the first of the month Thomas Foley, the father of [California governor] Gage's private secretary, would be made commissary."[23]

NOVEMBER 11, 1899

The Board of Prison Directors met at San Quentin and elected Thomas Wilkinson to serve as warden of Folsom Prison.[24] He filled the role left vacant by the death of the prior warden, Charles Aull, who died at age fifty on October 9, 1899.

Aull had been at Folsom for more than ten years, having been appointed in 1887, after a colorful career that included stints at San Quentin as well as a detective for the Wells Fargo Company. While Aull was in charge at Folsom, there were at least two significant escape attempts, with the most famous being in 1893, when seven inmates attempted to escape with the outside help of some members of their train robbing gang.

During this attempt, a fierce gunbattle ensued in the quarry at Folsom, with Warden Aull taking up arms himself and plunging into the fray, firing forty-five shots from a Winchester rifle.

A report from California prison directors in 1894 concluded a "24-foot wall around the prison grounds, including the quarries, would eliminate all chance of a recurrence of a similar break as that of June 27, 1893."[25]

DECEMBER 1, 1899

Thomas Wilkinson officially took over as "Warden of the State Prison at Folsom California for a term of Four (4) years, beginning on and dating from December 1st, 1899, as appears of record in the Official Book of Records of the said State Board of Prison Directors, on file in the said San Quentin Prison, under date of November 11th, 1899."[26]

He would serve for four years.

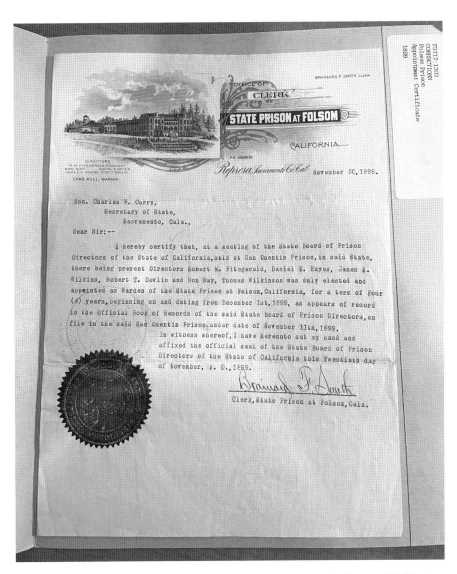

Thomas Wilkinson was elected warden of Folsom Prison, 1899–1903. *Courtesy of California State Archive.*

May 22, 1902

The beginning of the new administration at Folsom Prison was not without controversy, as Warden Thomas Wilkinson came under investigation[27] for numerous allegations, including tampering with inmate mail and excessive use of force, specifically related to the use of straitjackets.

According to an article in the *San Francisco Call*, "Information was lodged with the postal authorities that recently Warden Wilkinson went to a railroad station near Folsom and, intercepting a bag of mail before it was delivered into the hands of Postmaster Smith at Represa, which is the postal destination of all mail addressed to attaches and Inmates of the Folsom penitentiary, he opened it and extracted letters therefrom. Warden Wilkinson, according to the information given the postal authorities, took from the mail pouch several letters addressed, so it is said, to himself and then locking it up again he allowed it to be sent on to the Represa post office."

While the allegations of removing letters from the mail are troubling, even if they were addressed to him, it is the terrors resulting from use of "the jacket," including one inmate who was crippled and another who died as a result, that may have added to the coming boiling point.

> *Prisoner No. 469, James Dear, was placed in a straitjacket March 6, 1901, and when he was released eleven hours later, he was in a state of physical collapse. He was thrown into his cell, where he lay all night without medical attention. He died the following morning, and the autopsy showed his death to be due to congestion of the kidneys, liver, lungs, and brain.*[28]

Dear was not the only alleged victim of the horrors of the jacket during this short period of time. Other inmates were seriously injured, including one named Weitz, prisoner number 481, who was held in bondage for first twelve hours and then more than twenty-five hours continuously, resulting in permanent crippling of his hands. Another prisoner, Smith, number 1081, was kept bound for more than twenty-eight hours as punishment for neglect of duty.

The behavior against inmates was not the only complaint against Wilkinson, but they did all seem to be driven by his relationship with the guards. Beyond the abuse of inmates, and putting certain prisoners in positions of power, guards also alleged new policies that changed the quality of the sheets they were issued and forced them to pay for laundry done by prison workers, who, given the racism of the time, were almost exclusively Chinese.

JULY 16, 1902

Under Wilkinson, "trusty/trusties" were convicts who were given extra benefits in exchange for work done throughout the prison. According to reports, there were concerns among guards with trusties being given too much power and, in some cases, being encouraged to spy on and report on the behavior of the guards—or even try to give the guards orders.

According to a July 16 article in the *San Francisco Call*, in the prior thirty days, fourteen guards had resigned from Folsom Prison and said, "They were unable to serve the State by reason of the fact that Warden Thomas Wilkinson has given the convicts more privileges than the men whom he has engaged to guard them. The guards have had to receive orders from such 'pets' as Tom Fonte and other trusted spies of the Warden. Fonte is a convict of the worst dye, yet he was allowed to roam over the prison at will, issuing orders and acting more like a superior officer than a man who was suffering imprisonment for crime."[29]

The guards also complained of the quality of food they received, but when trusty Tom Fonte, who was serving a twelve-year sentence for robbery, led a plan to poison guards to effect a breakout for six men, it was too much. The plan was foiled, and all involved ended up in "the dungeon" on a diet of bread and water as punishment. Fonte had come close to springing multiple convicted felons, including "Bandit Jack Brady, a life termer; 'Kid' Thompson, a notorious train robber; Kris Myrtle, a desperate man; [and] Santonia Whiting, another 'bad man.'"

The administrators of California's prisons were surprised by the allegations and seemed to be unaware of any issues, saying none had been reported to them, with the press reporting,

> *R.M. Fitzgerald, president of the Board of Prison Directors, was astounded to read the article in* The Call *yesterday narrating the attempted outbreak at Folsom prison. In speaking of the matter, he said:*

"I was astonished beyond measure to read the revelation in The Call. *I have not in my official capacity received a report from Warden Wilkinson. If the outbreak is of the gravity reported, I assume that Warden Wilkinson should certainly communicate with me about It. The mode of procedure in cases of infraction of the rules which require the attention of the board is very simple. The Warden reports the matter to the Directors and the prisoners are called in to state if they are guilty or not of the charges made against them. If they deny guilt an investigation is held. At the conclusion of the hearing the board fixes the punishment, usually adopting the recommendation of the Warden as to the punishment advisable in each case."*[30]

JANUARY 7, 1903

George Pardee was inaugurated as California's twenty-first governor—and first born after California gained statehood—on January 7, 1903. Pardee was a medical doctor by training, with a focus on issues of the eyes and ears, having followed his father into the medical field. He also followed his father, Enoch, into politics, where Enoch had served terms in the state assembly and as mayor of Oakland. After beginning his political career with a successful election to the Oakland Board of Health, nineteen years later, George followed his father as mayor.

His medical background was timely, as California and especially the San Francisco Bay Area was under assault by an outbreak of the bubonic plague. The seriousness of the situation—as if the literal plague were not serious enough—was that the business community and specifically the Mercantile Joint Committee did not want to acknowledge the existence of the highly contagious fatal bubonic plague in the area, as it could have a negative effect on business.

Eventually, the business community acknowledged the plague and helped take action to curb its spread—but not before more than two hundred deaths were attributed to the outbreak. This was indicative of the ongoing friction in California between public policy, public health and the business community. California as a state began with the rush to plunder riches from the environment, tearing parts of the state apart in a breakneck attempt to acquire as much gold as quickly as possible with little to no regard for the effect on the environment, the Native people or one another.

Prison guards. *Courtesy of Folsom Historical Society.*

The impact or intrusion of commerce into public policy was seen during the development of both San Quentin and Folsom State Prisons, where contracts for prison labor were outsourced to private businesses as a way for the state to make money or offset the cost of housing prisoners. Whether this was sound policy for housing, not to mention rehabilitating prisoners, was not a factor, but there were interests who came to the state with proposals, and the state listened.

In his inaugural address to "Legislature and the People of the State of California," George Pardee addressed schools, hospitals and prisons, but only after he had already spoken on the "Protection of Industry" and "Irrigation and Water Laws," as well as the prosperous economic situation of California.

When he got to the section devoted to "Hospitals and Prisons," he grouped together those under the care of the state because of their actions and those protected by the state because of their conditions.

California, probably on account of her geographical position and her fame as a land of wealth and easy conditions of life, which serve as an attraction to the restless and idle, has an overplus of inmates in her penitentiaries and reformatories. These unfortunate persons constitute a small army of from 2,500 to 3,000 who are supported at an aggregate expense to the people of about $400,000 a year. There is another army of still more unfortunate ones, numbering over 5,000 who are inmates of our asylum-hospitals; and the burden of their maintenance is annually three quarters of a million dollars. In our two large Prisons, our five State Hospitals, and our Home for the Feeble-Minded, we are presented with problems enough to call for the efforts of the best penologists and alienists. May it not be proper to call to the aid of the State, to an extent greater than has yet been attempted, those who have made a scientific study of these matters and to get the benefit of their counsel and advice? [31]

This was followed by other sections on "Prison Government," and the "National Guard," both of which would become important topics to Pardee and those around Folsom.

In his address of prison government, Pardee seemed to acknowledge the state-appointed board for prisons could be doing more for reform and improvement, specifically related to the use of the congregate method, where all inmates, regardless of crime or age were grouped together.

The recent method of governing State prisons, through a Board of Directors, who are appointed for long terms, has brought forth some good results, and the Directors must be applauded for the improvements in discipline and the efforts toward the reformation of criminals which they have made. At the same time, it is admitted by the members of the Board, in their biennial reports, that there is room for changes for the better in a number of ways, most of which will require action by the Legislature. The congregate plan, by which persons of all degrees of criminality, old and young, first offenders and hardened veterans, are mingled, is still pursued.

There can be no doubt that this exercises a disastrous influence against the success of reformative measures. Both humane and economic reasons appeal to us to do what we can to bring our penal methods into line with the best thought of the day.

Later he addressed the necessity and value provided by the California National Guard in the face of concerns at the time regarding the danger of standing armies.

> *There can be no doubt that standing armies, such as are maintained by European countries, may be a menace to liberty, and certainly are expensive and a drag upon material prosperity. In our country they are not needed. On the other hand, the Spanish-American war has demonstrated the necessity of having a trained body of men ready to spring to arms whenever necessity shall demand. And the instant ease with which the National Government was able to put into the field armies of at least partially trained soldiers proved, beyond the question of a doubt, the necessity for an organization of State troops, through which passes a percentage of our young and patriotic citizens. It is idle to say that our National Guard is of no use.*

This prescience also was to be recalled in coming months as several companies of the California National Guard took to the field across the foothills and into the Sierras in pursuit of fugitives.

These topics, which continue to be of issue in California to this day, demonstrate the continuity of the big issues such as crime, confinement, drug use and law enforcement.

FEBRUARY 15, 1903

A report issued by the minority on the (California State) Assembly Committee on State Prisons and Reformatory Institutions referenced changes to discipline at Folsom State Prison, including bringing an end to the use of the straitjacket but not to other egregious punishments.

> *Since the discontinuance of the use of the straitjacket at Folsom the punishment, other than confinement in the dungeons, is by depriving the prisoner of his mail for a specified time, depriving him of credits and a more severe punishment of tricing or hooking up, which is done by placing the prisoner's hands behind him handcuffed and fastening them up at such height that he can just keep his feet on the ground.*[32]

The committee, or at least the minority of the committee, also built on the remarks from Governor Pardee's inaugural regarding changing California's approach to incarceration: "The minority of your committee believes that the whole present system and the law of this State affecting the punishment of criminals is radically defective and should be amended throughout. Your minority recommends that the aggregate system employed at the prisons should be abolished, and that a system should be adopted by which there should be a segregation of the men according to the most modern system adopted in penal institutions."

4

EARLY ESCAPES (1880–1903)

Folsom Prison was the scene of escape attempts almost from the beginning. These attempts included digging tunnels out from cells, getting help from someone on the outside and sometimes just walking away.

Following are looks at some of the more notable early escape attempts from Folsom Prison.

November 2, 1880

The "Foggy Walk Escape"

From November through March, when moisture from rain or ground meets rapidly cooling ground in the Central and Sacramento Valleys of California, a thick fog, called tule fog, is created. Early November in the area around Folsom has relatively mild weather with average high temperatures in the low seventies, while lows drop into the forties overnight. November 2, 1880, was extremely average with a high of seventy degrees and a low of forty-six. While there was no rain reported, there was enough moisture for a thick fog to form around Folsom.

Just a few months after the first prisoners arrived at Folsom from San Quentin, H. Northrup, prisoner number 27, took advantage of the lack of visibility and tried to walk away from a work crew into invisibility and freedom.

Since there were no walls, he walked through the fog and cold weather, twenty-two miles to Sacramento. If he'd kept walking, maybe he would have never been heard from again; however, Northrup wasn't able to resist a saloon or apparently causing trouble. He was apprehended a few days later after attempting to fight several other patrons and subsequently returned to Folsom in a "highly indignant frame of mind and spirit."[33]

December 11, 1889

The "Big Dig Escape"

Folsom Prison didn't have large exterior perimeter walls surrounding the buildings and yards until 1907. That didn't mean prisoners could walk out any time they wanted to, as they were often confined to cells or under the supervision of armed guards.

Four prisoners decided to try a different tack than making a run for it in their escape; they took their time, and they dug. Charles Geierman, C.H. Kohler and Tom Wilson were serving sentences of seventeen, ten and six years, respectively, for burglary, and Thomas Blumer was serving life for murder, and together they decided they needed to escape. They were going to do that by going under and through the prison.

Blumer and Kohler were cellmates in cell no. 20, as were Geierman and Wilson in no. 63, in cells on different tiers, or sections. During the night of December 11, they started their escape by cutting a hole in the granite floor of cell 20 using small tools they had smuggled in from the quarry where they worked during the day. Due to the rigid schedule, they had only one hour per night—from when they were locked in their cells at 9:00 p.m. to 10:00 p.m., when lights out was called, to dig. The time was so limited, and the tools were so small, they didn't break through the floor with a hole into a crawlspace for nearly three months, until March 17.

Once they were through the floor, they connected to the space underneath cell 63. The now four inmates would work together during the night digging first down six feet, and then toward freedom by getting beyond the prison, underground. Their work was slowed several times as they encountered bedrock and granite, through which they had to chisel their way through using short crowbars they had stolen from the quarry, and sneak into their cells by suspending them from twine around their necks and having them hang down into the legs of their pants.

The walls of the cellblock were supported by a foundation that "was laid at [a] depth of seventeen feet, the walls being eight feet in thickness at the base and tapering up to four feet at ground level, from which they were carried up at a thickness of two feet six inches."[34]

Five months after they first met up beneath cell 63, the four breathed fresh air when they emerged from the ground on the outskirts of the prison at 9:00 p.m. on August 18, 1890. After a wrong turn in the dark, when they headed to Orangevale to the west instead of Roseville to the north, they got on the right track and were soon headed away from Folsom. Among the few possessions with them was a five-dollar gold piece that they used to purchase clothes and food to help them on their way and to blend in rather than trying to hide in prison garb.

From Roseville, they headed east to Newcastle and through the foothills over the Sierra Nevada toward Reno and on another 30 miles to Wadsworth, Nevada. From Newcastle to Wadsworth is approximately 135 miles, which includes going over mountain passes of more than seven thousand feet, including Donner Pass, named after the ill-fated Donner Party, which became stranded there after an early season snowfall in 1846.

Just outside Wadsworth, they managed to catch a train that took them four hundred miles across the Nevada desert toward Ogden, Utah. Ogden was a transportation hub, with east–west and north–south trains meeting in the area, having been the closest town to the spot of the "Golden Spike," which completed the Transcontinental Railroad in 1869. Once in Ogden, the four found short-term employment digging ditches, but the pay wasn't enough. Soon some of the group fell into their old ways—which had gotten them locked up in the first place—and began stealing food from kitchens and clothes from clothing stores.

Eventually, their behavior caught up with them, and upon examination by the police, Kohler was found to have on him pictures showing himself in prison clothing and a clipping from a San Francisco newspaper documenting their escape.

The four prisoners were returned to Folsom Prison in early October 1890, ten months after they began digging in their cells. A reward of $200 per prisoner was paid to the chief of police of Ogden.

Following their return to Folsom, Kohler detailed the escape to prison officials, where "the confession of prisoner Kohler so astonished the directors that they pronounced the escape the most remarkable in the history of California."[35] As remarkable as the administrators may have thought the escape, there still needed to be an investigation and

Late 1800s guards. *Courtesy of Folsom Historical Society.*

consequences for the prisoners and for those who should have been watching them.

> *As a result of the investigation the directors decided that Turnkey Paul, who had been a trusted official of the prison for five years, had not shown proper vigilance in examining the cells of the escapers from time to time, and he was therefore ordered dismissed from the service....Paul offered no defense other than to say he thought he had been sufficiently vigilant. Guard Gerkner, who had charge of the tiers in which the cells of the escapes were located, was found guilty of a similar offense to that of Paul and was suspended from duty for two weeks.*[36]

June 27, 1893

The "Friends on the Outside Escape"

In 1890, William Fredericks was sentenced to three years at Folsom Prison after being convicted of robbing a stagecoach in Mariposa County, California. Mariposa is in the Sierra Nevada foothills about 150 miles south of Folsom and was one of the key areas in the California gold rush a few decades earlier.

He served his time at Folsom and was discharged but apparently made good enough friends with some fellow inmates to want to come back. These "friends" included George Contant, aka Sontag, member of a notorious train gang along with his brother John known as the Sontag Brothers; Frank Williams; Anthony Dalton; Charles Smith; Charles Abbott; and Henry Wilson.

Fredericks had promised Contant he'd help him escape and, through correspondence, agreed to purchase and surreptitiously deposit several guns on the grounds at Folsom.

In his memoir, *A Pardoned Lifer*,[37] Contant wrote about the layout and geography of Folsom Prison, some of which may not be accurate:

> *Folsom Prison, as many may not know, is situated one and one-half miles from the town of that name. It is the only prison in the United States which has no wall around it. It is in such a manner that nature has furnished barriers more effective than man could devise or construct.*
>
> *With the American River on one side, the other three sides protected by precipitous mountains, rising to an altitude of 400 feet, the opportunities offered a man to get out on his own resources are indeed meager.*
>
> *The American river [sic], to my notion, is the hardest river to cross in the world, for it took me over 15 years to get over it.*
>
> *The prison is constructed of huge granite blocks, in many instances several feet in thickness, which offer no means for digging out. The steel doors are the most powerful to be had, and the arrangements are such that when once behind them, there is no man who can hope to get out, except through the legal process.*
>
> *Monte Christo [sic], had he been penned up in this prison, would never have lived to wreak the vengeance, that followed his sensational escape from his lonely cell, depicted so luridly by Dumas.*
>
> *So, when any man attempts to break out of this prison, against such overwhelming odds—formed by a combination of nature and the hand of*

man—he is taking a mighty big contract among himself, and with one in a million chances of carrying out his intention.

It was in the quarry near the American River that Contant and his gang tried to make their escape. He used the cover of a pair of passing carts full of rock to hide from the section guard and then ducked into the powerhouse. The powerhouse was completed in 1893 and was the first hydroelectric powerhouse at a prison. The power was used to run the icehouse and provided electricity to various prison buildings and some businesses in Folsom.

The powerhouse is where Contant made his move. He made eye contact with another inmate in on the plan, who then passed on the signal to the others that it was on. He moved toward a guard, Lieutenant Frank Briare, and started a conversation just long enough for three others to come up from behind and overpower the guard.

Folsom Prison prisoners at work in forced labor at one of the quarries on the prison grounds. In California during this time, prisoners were often forced to work for the prison or as contractors hired out by the prison overseers for profit. *Courtesy of Sacramento Library, California Room.*

The commotion caught the eye of a guard in the tower who was manning a Gatling gun. The guard, Rigmore, fired a warning shot and voiced an alarm to the other guards. As the guards came to life, Frank Williams arrived with the guns that Fredericks had indeed come through with. The next few minutes were chaotic, as shots were fired, prisoners ran in every direction and some guards dropped to the ground as they were trained to do to get out of the way of the rifle and Gatling fire coming from the towers.

To get out of the quarry and off the prison grounds, the convicts had to climb a hill in the direct view of a guard who had set up a protected firing position behind boulders near the guard shack. From this position, he was able to take out prisoners as they made their break for freedom while also having the support of the Gatling gun, which rained down rounds on them.

In this maelstrom, Contant, who ended up taking seven bullets, and Abbott were both wounded by fire. Seeing the cause was lost, Conant placed his hat as a signal of surrender on top of the rock behind which they had sought shelter. After one last furious round of fire, they were approached by Warden Aull and Captain of the Guard R.J. Murphy, who commanded the guards to cease fire and the prisoners to raise their hands and drop the weapons.

At the end of the escape attempt, which had lasted about an hour, more than three thousand rounds had been fired by guards; four men, including Williams, Wilson and Dalton, were dead, along with inmate Thomas Schell, who had not been part of the escape attempt but was hit by stray fire; and no one had escaped.

WEAPONS OF FOLSOM PRISON

Guards fired a belt of ammunition the first day of each month "to keep it operational and for the psychological effect," according to the museum. It replaced a hand-cranked Gatling gun that was set at the prison boundaries to guard against mass escapes before the high stone walls were completed in the 1920s.
—Los Angeles Times[38]

There were four types of weapons at Folsom: weapons for the guards, weapons brought in from the outside, weapons made from something else and items used as weapons.

Weapons wielded by the guards at Folsom Prison ranged from handheld lead-tipped canes to early machine guns, with purposes running the gamut from intimidation to death. Lead-tipped canes were often carried by guards as tools to motivate inmates to action, to inflict pain as punishment or perhaps for the sadistic benefit of the guards. A standard cane would be a little more than three feet long, made of wood, with a curved handle for the hand at one end and a tapered tip at the other. With a lead-tipped cane, the tapered end is drilled out and filled with lead, adding weight and creating an effective weapon for one-on-one confrontations.

Another weapon for controlling inmates in close quarters was the "gas billy." These single-handed weapons were made of two parts: a tear gas dispenser and a short billy club. The billy club was usually nine to twelve inches long and may have been solid wood or leather-covered brass. The tear gas would be contained in a shell and dispensed through a choked

Guards armed with lead-tipped canes in the mess hall at Folsom Prison. On the tables are metallic mess kits to be used by inmates for meals. *Courtesy of Sacramento Library, California Room.*

barrel through a trigger so guards could let loose as much as necessary to control a situation.

At the other end of the spectrum were the big guns, meant as much to intimidate as for practical use. This included Gatling guns, which were hand-cranked machine guns with a series of rotating barrels that fired .45–70 caliber rounds at a pace of up to one thousand per minute, as well as actual cannons, including a six-pound brass howitzer. Folsom had several Gatling guns, including some 1877 "Bulldog" models that were manufactured at the Springfield Armory in Springfield, Massachusetts, and mounted on tripods and had five rotating cylinders to maximize the number of bullets they could dispense. The "brass howitzer" was likely actually made of lead or brass and was a cannon that fired a six-pound shot. These large weapons were in heavy use by the U.S. military for about twenty years from the Mexican-American War through the Civil War, when many were sold as surplus to other uses.

The powerful weapons were placed in towers around the property, where their multiple rounds of fire could be directed in several directions and wherever needed.

The weapon options for the prisoners were obviously a bit more limited than those of the guards and were usually modified or repurposed from items with different prescribed purposes, such as the heavy metal buckets that were kept to collect human waste overnight in prisoner cells that would sometimes be used as clubs or the razors that were necessary for grooming but also had sharp edges that could be put to other uses.

Other weapons started out as something else. Flat metal files were useful for many of the tasks required for jobs at Folsom Prison and were also easily smuggled out of workspaces and turned into deadly knives for cutting and stabbing.

6

HOW THEY GOT THERE

We are a civilized community here in California; we have civilized laws; we have civilized manners and civilized ways; we want no outlaws here.
—Judge E.C. Hart, 1901

Fred Howard, Fifteen Years, Robbery

Howard was almost paralyzed when the court pronounced the sentence. He had not counted on such a dose.
—Sacramento Union

In November 1897, Fred Howard was sentenced by Judge E.C. Hart to fifteen years at Folsom Prison for the robbery of the cash drawer and several customers at the B. Feraut's store. Acting with two others, Howard, who went by "Chicago Slim," was captured the next day and pled guilty, thinking this might give him an easier sentence. He was wrong.

Judge Hart said, "The crime of robbery is one of the most despicable denounced by our laws and one who engages in it has murder in his heart, for if a person upon whom the robbery is being committed resists, the robber is prepared to kill him, or to maim sufficiently to prevent the frustration of his plan. You have pleaded guilty and thereby have saved the county the expense of trying you for your crime. I have no doubt from the nature of the testimony adduced at the preliminary

Fred Howard, sentenced to fifteen years for robbery. *Courtesy of California State Archive.*

examination. which I have read, a jury would have convicted you. I have no sympathy for any man who will commit the crime of burglary. The judgment of the court is that you be confined in the State Prison at Folsom for the term of fifteen years."[39]

JOSEPH THERON, LIFE, ROBBERY

He did not doubt the mother's faith in her son, but…he was past reformation.

April 14, 1898

On the night of April 14, Joseph Theron, Henry Barker and Henry Staub "entered the store of Edward Leibschau at Mason and Pacific streets in San

Joseph Theron, sentenced to life for robbery. *Courtesy of California State Archive.*

Francisco and covered the proprietor with their revolvers. He resisted and they beat him into insensibility with their weapons and took all the money he had. When Leibschau regained consciousness, the police were summoned, and the criminals were captured."[40]

When Theron was brought to trial for his crime, his attorney pulled out all the stops to try to save him.

> *His counsel, Eugene N. Deuprey, put the lad's mother on the stand to testify as to his good character. The witness was an aged woman and told her story in a voice trembling with emotion. She said that she had two sons, one a seaman on the Charleston, the other the prisoner at the bar. Both were good boys, she said, and she asked the Judge if for her sake would he be not merciful. His Honor said that he did not doubt the mother's faith in her son, but he feared that she was mistaken as his record showed that he was*

past reformation and that he must suffer the punishment meted out to his accomplice, imprisonment for life.[41]

On June 20, 1898, Joseph Theron was transferred to Folsom Prison by Deputy Sheriffs Degan and Appel to begin a life sentence.

ALBERT SEAVIS, TWENTY-FIVE YEARS, BURGLARY

He robbed a store in Sacramento and will find that the California prison will keep him out of harm's way for some time to come.
—Carson Morning Appeal, *August 9, 1900*

August 7, 1900

Albert Seavis, a negro, who at an early hour last Saturday morning, held up and robbed a man named Julius Jansen at Front and K streets,

Albert Seavis, sentenced to twenty-five years for burglary. *Courtesy of California State Archive.*

and who was arrested a few hours later by Officer Michael Fisher today appeared in the Superior Court and entered a plea of guilty. Judge Hart sentenced him to twenty-five years' imprisonment in the penitentiary. Seavis was released from the Nevada penitentiary one week ago.[42]

Sacramento may have been Seavis's first stop after leaving Nevada following his release, as Sacramento is just 130 miles from Reno and the train corridor between the two was one of the first established in the western United States.

The newspapers in Nevada dutifully reported on Seavis's latest conviction: "Albert Seavis, colored, who was recently released from the Nevada Penitentiary, was sentenced to twenty-five years in the Folsom prison the other day by Judge Hart of Sacramento. Seavis robbed a Swede of his watch and money."[43]

In California in 1900, one of the most described features of a Black man was his race. With Albert Seavis, who had been in prison at least once before and was convicted of several crimes, that his race was the usual first descriptor said a lot about his perceived place in society.

RICHARD M. "RED" GORDON, FORTY-FIVE YEARS, ROBBERY

Robbery is only slightly less serious than murder.
—Judge E.C. Hart

February 4, 1900

Richard M. Gordon was sentenced to forty-five years imprisonment at Folsom for the February 4, 1900 robbery of John A. Mills near Capitol Park in Sacramento. He did not act alone and had Henry Spellman and A.B. Spellman with him, who, accounts[44] claim, were not brothers. Gordon was also identified as Harry Frier, or Freer, who had either served a term, escaped from a term or jumped parole at Joliet Prison in Illinois.

This group was suspected of several crimes, including the murder of a saloonkeeper and the shooting of a butcher, both in Oakland. In the case of their assault on Mills, they were annoyed at the small sum of money he had on him and brutally beat him when the amount he provided under threat wasn't as much as they expected. This was similar to their alleged murder of John Thomas at a bar in Oakland when they shot him during a robbery.

Perhaps to take the pressure off the investigation for other crimes, the three pleaded guilty to the assault with the hope of leniency from the presiding judge, Elijah Carson, or E.C. Hart. He started studying law at age thirty after an early career in newspapers, starting as an assistant to a printer at age twelve and eventually becoming a reporter, editor and finally publisher in Oroville, California. His transition from reporter to barrister was rapid, and following his beginning study of law in 1884, he was allowed to practice law the next year and then elected city attorney of Sacramento one year later. He then served in the state legislature until he was elected superior court judge of Sacramento County, where he served from 1897 to 1907 before serving twenty-two years as associate justice of the Third District Court of Appeal in Sacramento.

Richard M. "Red" Gordon, sentenced to forty-five years for robbery. *Courtesy of California State Archive.*

Whether he was being facetious or not, we cannot know for sure, but the judge said their act of contrition "strongly appealed to his magnanimity, and therefore instead of giving them life imprisonment, which he said they deserved," he sentenced Gordon to forty-five years at Folsom, as he said he considered robbery only a slightly less serious crime than murder.

RAY FAHEY, LIFE, ROBBERY

Citizens of this community do not want your kind of people here.
—Judge E.C. Hart

July 29, 1901

Ray Fahey arrived at Folsom Prison to begin serving a life sentence for a robbery in Sacramento. He appealed[45] his case, and it was affirmed on November 12, 1901.

Fahey was found guilty by Judge E.C. Hart of robbing A.L. Fortson, who was a telegraph editor at the *Record Union*, one of the leading newspapers in the Sacramento area with a circulation of more than fifty thousand. As telegraph editor, who would usually be responsible for writing copy based on the news that came in over the telegraph wire, Fortson would have been familiar with crime and punishment. As Fahey had not been long in the Sacramento area, he may have been surprised by the punishment he received, but according to comments from Judge Hart, the severity should not have been a surprise.

You and Enrleht evidently were strangers to this Jurisdiction. When you came here to ply your unlawful vocation you were evidently not familiar with the policy which has been established and followed by this court, of inflicting the severest penalty for offenses such as the one in which you are involved before the court now. It has been the policy of the court to show no leniency to a man who will go out into the dark and conceal his identity, stand in a corner with a weapon—a slungshot or something of that sort—for the purpose of striking and perhaps killing or shooting some citizen of the community—some honest, honorable citizen who works hard to accumulate the little that he has. If you had been familiar with the policy of this court on these questions, probably you would not have come here. Citizens of this community do not want your kind of people here. We are a

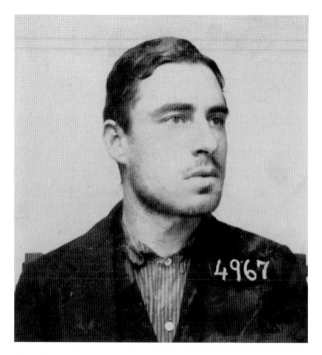

Ray Fahey, sentenced to life for robbery. *Courtesy of California State Archive.*

civilized community here in California; we have civilized laws; we have civilized manners and civilized ways; we want no outlaws here.[46]

EDWARD DAVIS, THIRTY-THREE YEARS, ROBBERY

The sentence practically amounts to life Imprisonment for Davis is nearly forty years of age. If he lives out the sentence twenty-seven years behind prison bars will leave him unfitted for continuing the role of footpad.
—San Francisco Call[47]

November 2, 1901

Otto Fleissner and R.N. Hamlin[48] were in San Francisco at the corner of Van Ness Avenue and Jackson Street at the edge of Pacific Heights and below Nob Hill at nine o'clock on a Saturday night when they were accosted by several men, with one of them holding a gun to Hamlin's head.

The next day, San Francisco police Detectives Crockett and Riordan apprehended Edward Davis on Minna Street, near where Hamlin rented rooms, having just recently arrived in the city.

Davis was quickly convicted and sentenced to thirty-three years.

FRANK CASE, LIFE, ROBBERY

I cannot make any bargain regarding sentences. You may have a trial if you want it you know. Do you plead guilty or not?
—Judge B.N. Smith[49]

January 14, 1902

E.E. Powers was an attorney in Los Angeles and partners with Christopher Franklin Holland in the firm of Powers & Holland[50] when he was going to visit a friend on Olive Street during the evening. It had been a warm day with temperatures reaching seventy-two degrees Fahrenheit in Los Angeles, but clouds had come in throughout the day and the temperature had dropped a bit. Between Ninth and Tenth Streets, Powers was accosted by three men. One had a revolver, another had a metal bar and the third took Powers's gold watch and thirteen dollars.

Just a few days later, the same three struck again on January 18, on Figueroa Avenue, when they took a gold watch, a gold chain and a twenty-dollar gold piece from Major E.F.C. Klokke. While these three seemed lucky with their success at larceny, they were unlucky in that they happened to walk past a man who had been a guard at San Quentin. This was important, as the three had recently come down from Northern California, where Frank Case had served two terms at San Quentin and was awaiting trial on highway robbery in the Alameda County Jail when he and William Kelly escaped the day after Christmas.

The former guard notified the local police, and when detectives followed up on the lead, they caught up with Case, Kelly and the third man, Chris Myrtle. All were apprehended, with Case and Kelly caught in a room at their boardinghouse and Myrtle at gunpoint in the street by Detective Kelly (no relation believed to William Kelly).

They knew they were in trouble when effects of the robberies were discovered in their room, and Case pleaded guilty to superior court judge Smith on February 7. He was sentenced to life.

Top: Edward Davis, sentenced to thirty-three years for robbery. *Courtesy of California State Archive.*

Bottom: Frank Case, sentenced to life for robbery. *Courtesy of California State Archive.*

Top: John H. Wood, sentenced to life for robbery. *Courtesy of California State Archive.*

Bottom: James Roberts, sentenced to twenty years for robbery. *Courtesy of California State Archive.*

JOHN H. "TEX" WOOD, LIFE, ROBBERY

*A man who holds a pistol to shoot will take life, therefore he ought
to have a life sentence.*
—Judge Cook

January 27, 1902

John H. Wood arrived at Folsom Prison to serve a life sentence for robbery. This sentence may seem severe until you consider he was convicted of a similar crime while serving as a soldier in the Philippines, where after deserting his post, he set upon travelers for highway robbery. He was convicted by a military tribunal and transported to San Francisco to serve his sentence in the military prison on Alcatraz.

Upon his release, he returned to a life of crime and used a handgun to rob a street merchant of a watch and chain.

> *Judge Cook who passed sentence on him took the position that a man who used a deadly weapon in the commission of his crime should receive the full penalty of the law. A man who holds a pistol to shoot will take life, therefore he ought to have a life sentence.*[51]

In response to his sentencing, Wood said, "That is an awful dose, and I haven't had my breakfast yet."

JAMES P. "SMILEY" ROBERTS, TWENTY YEARS, ROBBERY

He is "a weakling, mentally, and apparently harmless."
—Judge E.C. Hart

April 6, 1902

James P. "Smiley" Roberts arrived at Folsom Prison on April 6, 1902, to serve a twenty-year sentence for robbery. He, along with James Galley, was convicted of two muggings in San Francisco on the night of November 2, 1901. In the first, it was alleged they approached a waiter named Robert Clothier on the street, asking for the price of a meal, then attacked, choked and robbed Clothier of $2.10. After obtaining the money, at the point of a pistol, they encouraged their prey to walk away.

They then attempted the same with a plumber named Robert Dillistone a few blocks away. Dillistone, however, was able to break free and blew a police whistle to scare away his attackers.

Roberts, as were many at the time, was an opium addict and had only recently arrived in the area from Oklahoma. He and Galley were described as looking like hobos.

During their first trial, in February, on the charge of robbing Dillistone, the jury was unable to come to an agreement and entered a protest on the conditions of the jury room, noting:

> *We, the panel Jurors of this honorable court, respectfully enter a protest against being huddled in a small cubbyhole for a jury room. Our deliberations cannot be kept secret, as we are compelled to open the ventilators, and as a consequence our discussions cannot help but be heard by those passing along the corridor. We think our quarters should be condemned, and under the cubic air law would be. In the next place—we have no toilet accommodations. We are of the unanimous opinion that our present quarters are uninhabitable and respectfully request your Honor to bring the matter before the proper authorities in an endeavor to have these defects remedied at the earliest possible date.*

Judge Dunne made the following reply:

> *I can only say, gentlemen. In reply, that I have endeavored for the last eighteen months to obtain proper accommodations, and I think your statement here is a sufficient answer to those people who have believed that my own conduct was due to an obstinate feeling against coming here at all. That is quite untrue. I have at all times been ready to come here to this building if they would give me the proper accommodations. The jury is entitled to the same accommodations as the District Attorney or the court. They occupy the same position as the court in a way. Since they are the judges of the facts in every criminal case, and their position and jurisdiction, so to speak is coordinate, and that being the case they are entitled to proper accommodations. For such accommodations I have insisted, but it appears that a higher power has overridden me and has compelled us to accept insufficient and inadequate quarters. I am glad you have seen fit to make this protest, as I think it may be followed*

by a correction of the abuse, or at least I hope so: I trust, however, gentlemen, that no want of accommodations will prevent us from doing our whole duty.[52]

On March 29, 1902, Roberts was convicted of the robbery of Clothier and sentenced to twenty years at Folsom Prison.

John Joseph "J.J." Allison, the "Lone Kid," Four Years, Robbery and Second-Degree Burglary

They battered them almost out of recognition, nevertheless finally had to give up the attempt with nothing but the fine revolver to show for their night's work.
—Stockton Record[53]

December 29, 1902

In mid-December 1902, twenty-two-year-old John Joseph "J.J." Allison and Oliver Ross took a boat up the river through the Sacramento delta from San Francisco. They arrived on a Wednesday night and hooked up with a local, John Sullivan.

They wasted no time and went to work on a mini crime spree that started with breaking into a shop where they stole a sledgehammer and various wedges and chisels. They then took their ill-gotten tools and proceeded to the Hickinbotham Brothers hardwood and caning material factory, but they weren't there for the wood—they were after something bigger. One of the crew hid inside during

John Joseph "J.J." Allison, the "Lone Kid," sentenced to four years for robbery and second-degree burglary. *Courtesy of San Joaquin County Historical Society & Museum.*

business hours and then, later that night after everyone had left, let the rest of their gang in. First stop was ransacking desk drawers, where they found several guns. These were a good start, but they set their eyes on the safe and went to work.

They took the sledgehammer they had stolen and knocked off the handle of the safe and then took the punches and knocked the handle shafts in. They filled the resulting holes with nitroglycerine and tried to blow the safe open to get to the cashbox they knew was inside. The explosion was big enough to blow off the outer door of the safe and scatter debris throughout the office. What it wasn't big enough to do was open the inner door of the safe, where their objective was held. This must have enraged the three, as they attacked the sides and inner door with their sledgehammer and chisels before finally giving up and leaving with just the revolvers.

The next night, they continued preying on the local populace and held up a young man, Barnett, on the street, stealing a watch from him. They may not have gotten much and left a good enough impression for him to provide a partial description that led police to a nearby boardinghouse an hour later. Police then found the watch and missing guns buried in a nearby churchyard.

Three officers brought in John Sullivan, Oliver W. Ross and John Joseph Allison for robbery and second-degree burglary on December 29, 1902, at 3:30 p.m.

On January 7, 1903, Allison arrived at Folsom Prison to serve four years as prisoner 5281, with a term expected to expire on January 7, 1906. On his arrival, he was just twenty-two years old and stood five feet, nine and a half inches tall.

JOSEPH MURPHY, FOURTEEN YEARS, BURGLARY

Murphy has a bad record behind him.
—Contra Costa Gazette

February 25, 1903

Joseph Murphy was found "guilty of the crime of Burglary of the first degree and that he be punished by imprisonment in the State Prison of the State of California, at Folsom for the term of Fourteen Years. He was part of a group of nine men who robbed the home of Hermann Bendel."[54]

This may seem like an excessive sentence for burglary; however, this wasn't Murphy's first encounter with the law. According to the *Contra Costa Gazette* of February 28, 1903, when the paper covered Murphy's trial,

> *The attorney for the defendant, Leo Tormey, pleaded for mercy, but this had no effect on the court. Murphy has a bad record behind him. When arrested at Richmond for the burglary of the Grand hotel, he was placed in the local jail, and while there set fire to the structure. He was also a member of the gang who succeeded in effecting a break from the county jail.*

To break out, Murphy and two others, Frank Caldwell and Fred Smith, used surreptitiously acquired saws to cut through several thick iron bars that had been weakened with muriatic acid. They wrapped the saw blades in old clothes to try and deaden the sound of their cutting to freedom. When through the window, they dropped to the jail yard before climbing over the exterior wall using an improvised ladder made from a blanket, a mop handle, and a loop of wire used as a grappling hook to catch the top of the wall.

Climbing over a wall using a blanket may have been a challenge for Murphy who was described as being five feet six and half inches tall and weighing 235 pounds.

Joseph Murphy, sentenced to fourteen years for burglary. *Courtesy of California State Archive.*

HARRY "THE BORER" ELDRIDGE, THIRTY YEARS, ROBBERY

Until this trouble, I have led an honest life for the last five years.
—Harry Eldridge

March 31, 1903

By the time Harry Eldridge arrived at Folsom Prison at age forty in the spring of 1903, he had been in and out of prisons and jails for nearly half his life. His first long stint of prison appears to be a fifteen-year sentence at San Quentin for burglary, of which he served nine years from 1885 to 1894, but that wasn't even his first conviction. He also went by Harry Lorraine, and R., possibly Richard, Doel.

Eldridge was what was called a career criminal. His first conviction may have been as early as 1879 in Los Angeles when he was sentenced to two years for burglary when he was just sixteen. Apparently, that didn't have a rehabilitative effect on him, as he was then said to spend several years in San Francisco breaking into safes. His method was so consistent, and he was so prolific, he was referred to as "the Borer,"[55] for his way of drilling into safes.

While he never pleaded guilty to being the Borer, the thefts stopped while he was in San Quentin. Following his incarceration, he married and seemed to be leading a straight life, which fell apart when his wife left him after five years for a visit back east. He turned back to crime, with several burglaries in Oakland having similarities to past Borer crimes, both in methodology and with a focus on stealing silver. His luck again ran out after he broke into the home of Thomas Coghill at 1514 Jackson Street just a few days after Christmas in 1902 and stole $300 worth of silverware. Two detectives, Ryan and O'Dea, were assigned to the case and learned the booty had been pawned in Oakland and homed in on one of the usual suspects.

The house on Jackson Street wasn't just any house; it had been built in 1877 as an investment by Samuel Merritt, one-time mayor of Oakland, founder of a namesake hospital, University of California Regent, referred to as "the father of Oakland parks, and the builder of the 12th street dam which created Lake Merritt,"[56] and was three stories with bay windows, a large porch and dome-shaped peaks.

The house was then bought in 1880 for $12,500 by San Francisco attorney John Stanley as a wedding gift to Catherine, his daughter, and

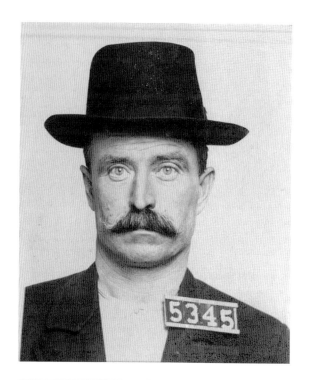

Top: Harry Eldridge, sentenced to thirty years for robbery. *Courtesy of California State Archive.*

Bottom: Frank Miller, sentenced to twelve years for robbery. *Courtesy of California State Archive.*

her husband, a grocer, Thomas Coghill. If Harry Eldridge was looking for a target likely to have silver and jewels, which were his preferred plunder, this was the right house. If he was looking for an easy mark where he could get away, he chose poorly.

Following his conviction, he implored superior court judge John Ellsworth for leniency by exclaiming, "Your honor, until this trouble I have led an honest life for the last five years. I am married to a wife I dearly love and have a son to whom I am sincerely attached. They need my support and protection."[57] The sixty-one-year-old jurist was not new to the law, having spent ten years as Alameda city attorney,[58] then several terms in the state legislature, before taking his seat in the judge's chair in 1889.

He was unmoved by Eldridge's sentiment and sentenced him to thirty years at Folsom Prison.

FRANK "THE LITTLE DUTCHMAN" MILLER, TWELVE YEARS, BURGLARY, FIRST DEGREE

He frequented the worst resorts and kept company with crooks constantly.
—San Francisco Call

April 25, 1903

Frank Miller arrived at Folsom Prison from Fresno to serve a twelve-year sentence for first-degree burglary. He was convicted with three others of breaking into the Louis Einstein and Co. Store in Fresno on January 6, 1903, and stealing $2,000 worth of items, including a hunting knife, a suitcase, a shotgun and three revolvers.[59] They also stole bolts of expensive silk.

The four were arrested in San Francisco in late January when their rooms at 158 Fifth Street were raided by police. In the room were several items from the theft in Fresno, including the silk, which still had labeling from the Einstein store. This raid was driven by suspicion that they had also been involved in a burglary at the Buffalo Brewing Company on King Street in San Francisco, where they blew open the safe. San Francisco police had been on the lookout for the crew after receiving a circular shared by Fresno's Chief of Police Morgan and Sheriff Collins.

7
THE DIE WAS CAST

They had my father and Captain Murphy in the Captain's office and were cutting them to pieces with knives.
—Albert Wilkinson, 1903

July 26, 1903

Prisoners M. Murray and Porfirio Alviso worked in the rock quarry at Folsom, as did many of the inmates. On this Sunday afternoon, Red Shirt Gordon asked Alviso if he had access to blasting caps and fuses, as he Gordon apparently had dynamite.

There is no record if Alviso complied with Gordon's request, but there is a record of him taking his concerns with it to Murray, who then took it to Lieutenant Kipp at about 2:30 p.m. "and laid the facts before him, but Lieutenant Kipp did not seem to think the story had any foundation and did not investigate it."[60]

Both of the reporting inmates had spent a considerable amount of time at Folsom, with Murray, inmate no. 2070, arriving in 1889 and at the time fourteen years into a forty-year sentence for murder, and Alviso was received in 1895 after being sentenced to fifteen years for robbery in San Luis Obispo County.

An explosion in the quarry at Folsom Prison that may have been detonated as part of the removing of stone. *Courtesy of California State Archive.*

JULY 27, 1903

July 1903 was a time of turbulence and change across America and throughout the world. On July 9, in Pennsylvania, Charles Kruger shot and killed Constable Harry Foster "Darby" Bierer, who had come to arrest him. On July 20, 1903, Pope Leo XIII died, and many newspapers for the next week carried news of his passing and the upcoming conclave to select a new pope. On July 23, the first Ford Model A was sold in Chicago, beginning the age of the automobile in a world still dominated by horse travel, and at least two lynch mobs took to the streets in search of misguided vigilante justice in towns from Basin, Wyoming, to Danville, Illinois, and left death and destruction in their wake.

Days at Folsom were long and full of hard work and monotony. The activities and actions of prisoners were the same, day after day. The day began with an early wake-up call. William Grider was likely still getting used to the routine at Folsom, having arrived just a few months earlier, on May 5, to serve a five-year sentence for burglary in the second degree. At some point during the prior night, or when they woke up, he learned from his cellmate Harry Eldridge there was going to be a breakout, possibly that day.

After waking up, convicts would then step outside their cells with their night buckets and empty them in the slot in the floor that ran through the middle of the cellblock.

After their night buckets had been emptied, the prisoners headed to breakfast. It was around this time that Grider made the choice to tell a trusty what he had heard from his cellmate.

After breakfast was time for work, and in 1903, this would have included working in a prison business, where convicts would labor long days for extremely little or no pay. There were several businesses at Folsom in 1903, but the primary enterprise was the quarry, as it had been from day one. To get to the quarry, inmates walked in single file from the cellblock through the yard and down the hill.

On Monday, July 27, as on most Mondays at 7:00 a.m., there was "court," in the office of the captain of the guard, R.J. Murphy, who had worked at Folsom for twenty-three years. The warden, Thomas Wilkinson, would sometimes sit in while prisoners who had committed infractions were adjudicated. The office had several rooms, with an entryway and the main office in back. There was a white line, a dead man's line, painted on the ground at the entrance to the office yard and about twenty feet from the door that was not to be crossed by inmates until they were summoned. If an inmate crossed this line, they could be killed, immediately. Those who had to answer to the court for anything ranging from fighting to talking back would fall out of line on the way to their prison job and form a single file in front of the office.

Near the office that day were Guards W.C. Chalmers, William Cotter and Charles Jolly and general overseer Joseph Cochrane. "Cochrane was known among inmates as 'The Chaw.' He was a fearless officer, a stern disciplinarian; yet beneath his rough exterior possessed a kindly nature, and was known to the convicts as 'square,' which in prison parlance means that he was the type of official who would not tolerate unfair treatment being meted out by those under his authority."[61]

While "court," was getting started, "Alviso and Murray, immediately on their arrival at the rock-crusher, about 7 a.m., approached Foreman C.I. Taylor and communicated the fact of the request made by Gordon," who had asked about blasting caps for dynamite.

Back at "the court," inmates lined up in the growing heat of the day. Although it was still early in the day, forecasts showed temperatures might be above average and indeed possibly one of the hottest days in the history of Folsom Prison.

Guard tower with Cochran. *Courtesy of Folsom Historical Society.*

At the head of the line was "Red Shirt" Gordon. Prisoners who were marked as incorrigible were required to wear red shirts, one of the few "uniforms" that the cash-strapped state provided. Behind Gordon, who was serving forty-five-years for robbery, was Edward Davis, also in for robbery

The prison yard was the primary outdoor recreation venue for inmates at Folsom Prison. In this photo you can also see the parts of the cellblock, administration building, and gate. *Courtesy of Sacramento Library, California Room.*

but in his case thirty-three years. Davis was reading a book in line, which seemed odd to Guard William Cotter, and this, coupled with Red Shirt Gordon in front of the line, caught his eye. Cotter was about to make a move to mix up the line when Davis's book slammed shut.

At the signal, all the prisoners in line produced a range of horrific weapons and burst forward into the office. There were knives made from files taken from the woodshop that had been sharpened and several razors taken from the prison barbershop.

At the front of the violent throng was Joseph Murphy, who made a beeline for Warden Wilkinson, who was sitting in a chair.

Guy Jeter, the foreman of the stone quarry at Folsom Prison, was in a chair in the office, and when the prisoners made their move, he stood up and struck Joseph Murphy over the head with a cane he had in his hand. His action caused some of the prisoners to turn their attention to him, and he was grabbed from behind and thrown against the wall at knifepoint before being pushed into the next room with the command, "Damn you, get into that office."

Guard Cotter was already moving and picked up a chair and swung it back and forth to try to stem the tide into the office, but he was cut down with multiple stab wounds and slashes, which both Eldridge and Murphy credited to Andy Myers, another convict. Cotter was not the only one to fall, as Joseph Cochrane was sliced multiple times while he waded into the fray swinging his lead-tipped cane and shouting, "Throw up your hands!"

Guard Cochrane kept fighting through the office, and the convicts' attention turned to him as knives flashed. Then a chair wielded by convict Murphy came crashing down on his head, and Cochrane went down to the floor, where he was stabbed several times. He tried to raise himself up against his attackers but eventually sought refuge under a high desk in the corner. His need to hide may have been related to him being a target, as he was blamed by some inmates for being the one who laced up the straitjackets, and "every man that got near enough put a knife in him."[62]

The warden, who was in attendance with his young nephew, was cut with a razor, although it may have only caught his clothes; it was apparently enough to wither his resolve. At least he thought it only caught his clothes. Guard Murphy tried to escape to another room, but Red Gordon stopped him with threats to cut his heart out.

Guard Chalmers went down as two prisoners fell on him while the others broke for the interior door. The attack may have come from Andy Myers and William A. Leverone, who, according to some, were also the two responsible for the injuries to Cotter.

Not all the nearby prisoners took part in the escape attempt, and some may have even fought against their fellow convicts who were looking for freedom.

The mêlée was relatively short, but brutal, and fought in close quarters with primitive weapons, leaving blood smeared, furniture scattered and dead and wounded in the office. Cotter, who had been a guard for seven years, had his hands over his midsection, trying to staunch the flow of blood after receiving enough cuts to essentially disembowel him. Before succumbing, he said, "He has killed me," then died on the floor of the office.

Charles Jolly was bleeding profusely from at least two stab wounds, as was Cochrane, who was taken by the convicts as a hostage.

In a quick council among the convicts, all acknowledged the "die was cast," with the killing of Guard Cotter. There could be no thought of turning back—it was to escape or face the hangman's noose. The warden was jerked to his feet by Gordon and told of their decision. He was given the choice of cooperating or dying where he stood. Warden Wilkerson [sic] agreed to cooperate if none of the hostages were harmed. Gordon assured him no one else would be hurt if he did as he was told.[63]

Now it was 7:38 a.m., and it wasn't enough to attack the guards; they were the ticket out, but first one more stop. The armory. Near the office was the armory, the secure room where dozens of weapons for the guards were kept.

With the tables turned and the guards now prisoners and serving as human shields, they were marched across the yard under the barrels of Gatling guns, which could fire eight to nine hundred rounds per minute. But when most needed, the guns were silent, as the guards in the towers quailed before the sight of their warden having a knife held to his neck, and "thirteen of the convicts then forced the warden and Captain Murphy to give a signal from the yard to the guards in the gun posts not to shoot."[64]

Prison Yard. *Courtesy of Folsom Historical Society.*

The armory was at the base of one of the guard towers, but the door was locked and the guards inside were showing stronger resolve than those in the tower and didn't immediately open the locked door. This resolve weakened when confronted with threats of dynamite backed up with the display of three sticks in a satchel. If Alviso and Murray were to be believed, these lacked the necessary fuses and blasting caps to be of any use, but no one at the door knew that.

The impasse ended when, under request from Warden Wilkinson, Lieutenant of the Guard Henry Kipp, who despite his fifteen years of service as a guard had earlier not thought the idea of a prisoner with dynamite important or likely enough to pass on to his superiors, either opened the door or provided a key to the escapees. If it was not Kipp, it may have been either Guard Glease, who was in charge of the armory and stationed on top of the tower that housed it, or Guard Hopton, who had control of the door. While the inmates were at the door, Wilkinson, Murphy and Kipp ordered the guards not to fire.

With the door opened, the brazen crew sidestepped Hopton, who had a gun in his hands but orders not to fire, and helped themselves to "ten Winchester repeating rifles, fifteen or twenty revolvers, and a quantity of ammunition," by breaking into lockers before destroying the rest of the weapons they didn't take, hopefully to slow the armed response after them. The total time at the armory was less than ten minutes.

Keeping several hostages, the prisoners kept moving toward freedom but were slowed by the severely injured Cochrane, who collapsed from exhaustion, and "one of the convicts stepped out of the line and violently kicked him in the abdomen, as he lay on the ground practically dying."[65] That may have been the end of Cochrane, if an inmate named Albert Seavis had not stepped out of the crowd of convicts and intervened and said, "No, sah, yu'all ain't gwine kill 'The Chaw,' no sah, yu'll ain't gwine kill him."[66] This briefly caused the escapees to turn their wrath on Seavis, until it subsided and he then joined their crew.

The interior gates of the prison were still open, and there was a very real danger of a general break with all prisoners going on the lam until Joseph Casey,[67] a trusty who was serving life for murder, slammed shut the inner door, preventing other inmates from making a break. While Casey was preventing further mayhem, another prisoner, O.C. Clark, made his way to the warden's office and raised the alarm, with a call to the city of Folsom, as a loud siren began to sound.

Prison yard with hill. *Courtesy of Folsom Historical Society.*

Clark was a "trusty in the captain's office, and as soon as he could get out of the office he gave a general alarm, phoned to Folsom for an extra doctor, assisted in caring for Guard Cotter and Turnkey Cochrane, and rendering every assistance that he could." He had been at Folsom Prison for almost seven years so far and was well into his sentence of twenty years for forgery.

With no walls to slow them and hostages as shields, the former prisoners and now escapees set out for freedom, which took them through the prison orchards. At the edge of the peach orchard, about a half mile from the prison but inside of the fence, the prisoners changed clothes with their captives. They then headed through the fence and overland until they came to the main road and toward the South Fork of the American River.

By late summer, the American River is a shell of its former self. In spring, powered by runoff of melting snow directly east in the Sierra Nevada, this portion of the river could run high, fast, bitingly cold and dangerous, but by the end of July, it has slowed to a trickle, and the water, while not warm, isn't going to take your breath away.

Not all the prisoners who started the assault made it to the river. Myers and Leverone may have had second thoughts after hearing gunshots and returned to the prison through the gate.[68] The gunshots likely came from Guard Thomas Ryan, who was following the group to see which direction they were going and wanted to signal where he was.

There was a stage line that ran the roughly twenty miles from Folsom to Coloma, where gold had first been discovered, and crossed over the river at Mormon Island with a bridge that had been built and washed away several times since 1850. On this sunny summer morning, it was standing for this crew on the run to cross. The group that crossed only vaguely resembled those who had crested the hill leaving Folsom under the eyes of the Gatling guns. The escapees had changed clothes with their hostages, swapping guard uniforms and suits for prison clothes.

Now that the hostages had gotten them beyond the guns and supplied them with a change of clothes, their usefulness was wearing thin. There was talk of executing the hostages, with Albert Seavis reportedly wanting to "shoot the top of his [guard Charles Jolly's] head into little bits,"[69] but calmer heads—led by Gordon, who said there was to be no murder, including the one they called "Dirty Dick" (Murphy)—prevailed, and hostages started being released. First Murphy and the younger Wilkinson were released about a half mile past the bridge to begin walking back. They were followed by Ward the mechanic and Guard Jolly, who was seriously injured and had just received a second chance at life due to the intervention of Frank Case, who was apparently more interested in getting away than murder.

When Captain Murphy returned to Folsom and spoke with the press, he said, "It is possible that Gordon may get away but he is such an ugly-looking fellow that anybody who has ever seen his picture would be sure to identify him."[70] What Murphy may not have known was that Red Shirt Gordon might have broken away from the group to try to make his way on his own shortly after he was released. He advised the rest of the group to do the same to make it harder for them to be followed, but some thought there was safety in numbers and decided to stay together.

From Mormon Island, the foothills begin to rise toward the mountains above the South Fork American River canyon, and the escapees were likely realizing they needed to move faster than their legs would carry them if they hoped to outrun the posses that had to be forming and already on their way. Their luck improved when they came upon Joseph Foster, who was driving a wagon with a team of four horses. They took Foster and his horses' hostage and compelled them to come with them on their run.

They continued toward Bear Mountain until they encountered another unfortunate traveler, Dan Schlottman, who was trying to get home with a load of wood. The heavy load would slow them down, so the hostages were put to work throwing Schlottman's hard work out on the road. Now with the horses from Joseph Foster's team added to the wagon they had just appropriated, the escapees changed course for Pilot Hill, likely following Pilot Hill Road.

The decision to continue was a given for Wood, who, in conversation with Allison, Theron, Eldridge and Murphy, made known that he did not plan on being taken alive. If he had the chance, he was going to go after any posses or militias that came after them and hopefully kill a few.

By now there were about twenty in the group, including thirteen escapees, six or seven guards they hadn't released and the unfortunate travelers Foster and Schlottman they'd picked up along the way.

The escapees may have moved a bit more swiftly if they understood how many were now in pursuit. There were no fewer than four posses on their trail that first afternoon, including two companies, Company C and H, from the second regiment of infantry in the National Guard of California, Sheriff Bosquit of El Dorado County with sixteen men, and Deputy Sheriff Edward Reese of Sacramento County with Deputies Wittenbrock, Haggerty, Hunters and Kilgore. All these posses were heavily armed and ready to fight.

While the posses fanned out across the countryside, there was still drama at Folsom as the wounded guards fought for their lives. Guard Cotter and Turnkey Cochrane, who were grievously injured, were being assisted by an unlikely source. Charles Abbott, who was twenty years into a life sentence for murder, assisted Cotter in the last minutes of his life before he succumbed to his injuries and carried Cochrane into the captain's office, where his wounds could be tended. He may have done this with a hope of redemption, as he had been part of an earlier escape attempt, although not as successful as this one.

8

ON THE RUN

*These men had better keep away from Sacramento. We know them, and the first
one who enters the city limits will get a mighty warm reception.*
—Chief Sullivan, Sacramento Police Department, 1903

July 28, 1903

Back at Folsom, there were already fingers being pointed trying to figure
who knew what when.

> *District Attorney Seymour and the prison officials had one of the cellmates of
> Harry Eldridge, one of the escapes, before them yesterday* [July 28, 1903].
>   *They declined to give the name of this convict. From him they learned
> that he had told a trusty that something was wrong with the men, and he
> had better warn the lieutenant of the day watch. The trusty told this convict
> to report the matter to Guard Cochrane, but he was unable to do so because
> Eldridge and Woods kept at this side afterward.*
>   *Eldridge and Woods were among the first to get out of the line and make
> the attack on the office of Captain of the Guard Murphy.*
>   *Eldridge's cellmate told the officers at the examination yesterday afternoon
> that last Sunday night Eldridge questioned him about the country in which
> the escapes have sought refuge. This occurred after the prisoners had all been
> locked in their cells for the night.*

Eldridge showed his fellow convict two rifle balls which he had, and said he was to have received more of them, but the person who was to have brought them got "cold feet."

Eldridge told his cellmate that he was going to "get out" and asked him to join with him. He told Eldridge he would have nothing to do with any jail break, and said Eldridge was foolish to attempt it.

Eldridge then pulled a knife from under his shirt and threatened to kill his fellow prisoner if he ever said a word to any free man about what he had told him.

The next morning Eldridge watched his cellmate closely, but the latter managed to hastily impart a word of warning to a trusty, advising him to tell Lieutenant Kipp of the threatening danger, but the trusty did not pay any attention to the warning, telling the prisoner to notify Guard Cochrane.

The prisoner said that if Eldridge saw him talking to a free man, he would kill him. Eldridge and Woods came up to the former's cellmate, and he had no further chance to talk to the trusty. They both asked what he had said, and he replied that he had been talking about going to work on the rock crusher. They kept him by them until the men formed in line to go out to work when the assault occurred.

Suspicion is directed to a convict named Smalding as one who assisted in perfecting the plans for the escape. The officials are quite sure he placed dynamite so the conspirators could get it. This is the dynamite with which it was intended to blow up the armory post if the guards made a fight.[71]

July 29, 1903

While the escapees were still making their way across the countryside, their victims started being laid to rest.

"William L. Cotter, the guard who was killed at Folsom prison, was buried in this city (Sacramento) today. A large number of friends of the deceased were in attendance. The guards of Folsom prison sent two beautiful floral pieces."[72]

One the same day Cotter was laid to rest, there was a search of William Leverone's cell by Guard Cary, who "discovered a shirt of Leverone's from which several pieces had been cut, on which there were blood spots, and these pieces had been thrown in the waste can. Blood was also discovered on the back of the shirt plainly showing he had participated in the assault."[73]

9

THE BATTLE OF PILOT HILL

There is twelve convicts and ten free-men who broke out of Folsom this morning,
and we had to kill a couple of men to get out, and we are up against it, and we
want our dinner as soon as we can get it.
—John H. Wood

July 27, 1903, 2:00 p.m.

Between 2:00 p.m. and 3:00 p.m., several hours after they had first leaped across the deadman's line, the group reached the small settlement of Pilot Hill, which consisted of a few small houses and the Pilot Hill Hotel, a combined hotel, store and post office that was operated by Sanford Diehl and his family. Pilot Hill is about seventeen miles from Folsom, following the path of the South Fork American River.

The Pilot Hill Hotel was a three-story wooden building with six narrow columns in front that supported a second-story porch and roof above that. There were four sash windows across the front that looked across the narrow porch, with two on each side of the main door. The porch had two steps that ran the whole length, making entry and egress from the wide approach easy.

A four-horse wagon being driven by Joseph Foster pulled up in front, and four men, including Wood and J.J. Allison, approached the porch.

It was on this porch that the proprietor stood with his back to the door; he was told by Wood that he would be providing the group with something to eat, and it was better he helped than be forced.

Wood said, "There is twelve convicts and ten free-men who broke out of Folsom this morning, and we had to kill a couple of men to get out, and we are up against it, and we want our dinner as soon as we can get it."

Diehl hadn't been planning on serving a midafternoon meal and let them know the fire was out and it would take a little time to get the food ready.

They took advantage of the situation and made time to eat from the hotel kitchen, as well as smoke cigars from the owner's personal stash. They spread out, with some escapees guarding the road that led up to the hotel, and others dispersed throughout rooms looking out the windows. While they were on guard, they were also very happy to be out. According to Guard John Klenzendorf, who was one of the hostages, "The convicts were in a jubilant state of mind. They sang and danced and shouted with glee."

As the convicts were spread out, the innkeeper, Diehl, kept an eye on some in the store, while his wife served others in the dining room. There was an attempt at an odd semblance of normalcy during the respite, with Wood recommending Diehl charge the cost of food to the state and making the hostages sign a receipt for the food they had. While he was talking with Diehl, and after he was done eating, Wood sat on a box and talked with the proprietor about the escape and the treatment he had received at Folsom Prison. Then, according to Diehl, Wood "asked me (Diehl) if I had a pair of field-glasses and I told him no, but he says, 'yes you have,' and I knew that he had seen them sitting on the clock-shelf in the dining room close to the table; and knowed that there was no use, and so I told him that I had a pair but that I did not want to lose them, and he says, 'Go and get them,' and I went out and got them and gave them to him."[71]

A fence about three feet high ran outward from each end of the porch, with pickets spaced about a foot apart, framing the front of the building as the 5:00 p.m. stagecoach that ran from Auburn to Placerville pulled up to the front. The stage ran every day, and the driver was probably used to answering questions but may have been surprised when he was greeted by a large group of heavily armed men and asked if he'd seen any posses on his way over. Apparently, his reply that he had not was satisfactory, as he was allowed to go on his way, which led to him possibly being able to alert others to the presence of something peculiar happening in Pilot Hill. Word of the breakout may not have reached him prior.

Following the scheduled stage, a wagon with three occupants approached the Diehls' place. A man, woman and child stumbled into the middle of the escape, much as the stagecoach driver had, and were asked if they had seen any posses and also responded in the negative. If the group was trying to be unobtrusive, this repeated line of the questioning was probably not helping.

Perhaps persuaded by the continued appearance of visitors and being still a relatively short distance from the scene of their escape, it was determined it was time to move on and the hostages were loaded back into the wagon, which was still driven by Joseph Foster, who was now several hours into his confinement. In high summer, the sun doesn't set in the Sierra foothills until well after 8:00 p.m., and when this motley group left Diehl's hotel sometime after five o'clock, the sun was still well above the horizon, and the temperature was probably still scorching.

Before the outlaws left, Diehl followed them to the wagon and bravely asked for his field glasses back, with Wood responding, "My friend I would like to accommodate you, but I can't do it for I need them in my business."[75]

There was continued disagreement among the escapees on whether to keep the hostages as continued leverage or turn them loose so they could move faster and unencumbered. They left at least one hostage who was sick behind at Diehl's. Contemporary reports, which may have been influenced by the racism of the times, say that Albert Seavis was in favor of executing all the prisoners, as he was referred to in several articles as the "Bloodthirsty Negro," the only escapee to be described in language like that.

With a group this large and likely full of strong personalities, there would have been many ideas on actions and directions to take. Complicating matters were the relatively few established roads in the area and also the needs of some of the escapees, which ranged from wanting to see women to having to get a fix to satisfy their opium cravings, to which at least two of the escapees were said to be addicted.

The disagreement may have been cut short when they were set upon about a mile south of Diehl's. The group was in at least one wagon and with several horses when they started receiving fire from an ambush set up by a posse made up of Folsom Prison guards and sheriff deputies.

Everyone scattered, but J.J. Allison, who was called, the "Lone Kid" while at Folsom Prison, stayed in the wagon. This was a poor choice, as he received a nasty gunshot to the abdomen. The pain must have been incredible. According to Joseph Murphy, Allison asked his companions to shoot him to end his pain, but they either couldn't or wouldn't, so he took matters into his own hands and said, "Goodbye pals," before shooting himself.

Beyond the mortally wounded Allison, most of the others bailed out of the wagon, with the escapees ordering their prisoners to wave a white handkerchief, saying, "Wave a handkerchief to them fellows to stop shooting."

Along with Allison, the wagon horses didn't survive the ambush, and the group was now on foot. Either during the battle or immediately after, Klenzendorff escaped, and the remaining hostages—Guards McDonough, Dolan, Hopton and Seavy and wagon drivers Foster and Schlottman—were released.

With his freedom, Klenzendorff went back to Pilot Hill. There, according to his testimony,

> [I] *went just a little distance the other side of the hotel and stopped. I met a lady there at the house, she came out and asked me if I was one of the prisoners, and I said "No, I am one of the free-men," and I asked her where the nearest telephone was; she told me it was about four miles, and she says "What do you want to do," and I told her I wanted to telephone Captain Murphy to tell my wife that I had got away safe and was not hurt. I staid [sic] there may be [sic] half an hour. I don't know what the lady's name was; I didn't inquire or introduce myself at all; I had something else to think about, about that time. I told her my name, I did not ask her name, nor did I ding out afterwards. After I went there, and told her who I was and what I wanted, she took a mule that was hitched to a buggy and drove to the telephone office and telephoned Captain Murphy, and I went back to the hotel, and when I got to the hotel there was a number of different men standing around there; and then we went out to identify this man* [Allison] *that was shot.*[76]

With the hostages all released, it was just the escapees and growing numbers of posses chasing them through the foothills.

The different ideas on where to go and different needs led to the group breaking up into at least two bands, with one group, the Manzanita Gang, heading east toward the Sierra Nevada and Reno; another, the Sacramento Gang, veered west towards Sacrament, and then more south.

There were side conversations and differing reasons on why and how the group split up, with some of the reasons maybe focused on destination or direction and others on groups of friends.

Roberts indicated he was inclined to stay with Howard.

The Sacramento Gang likely included Red Gordon (if he had not already left), Davis, Roberts, Case, Fred Howard, Albert Seavis and Ray

Fahey. At least three (Gordon, Seavis and Fahey) in this group had one thing in common: they had been sentenced to Folsom by Judge Hart. This led Sacramento police chief Sullivan to place guards around Hart's home, and he commented to a reporter,

> *I have made such arrangements that it will be impossible for any man to assault Judge Hart. I have taken due precautions to guard him. I do not know how the story originated that Gordon intended coming to Sacramento to take revenge upon the Judge who sentenced him to imprisonment. I don't think Gordon intends to do anything of the kind. If he or any of his fellow escapes head this way, I don't think they will dare to come any farther than the vicinity of Roseville, where they will be likely to board a night train for the north and then probably seek the Klondike country. These men had better keep away from Sacramento. We know them, and the first one who enters the city limits will get a mighty warm reception.*

Chief Sullivan wasn't too far off in his assessments of what the prisoners might do, as at least one of the escapees ended up on a train near Roseville and another went north, possibly heading to the Klondike or at least as far as Seattle.

Opium had come to California in the 1850s with immigrants from China who came to work in industries around the search for gold or to search for gold itself. In 1903, opium wasn't illegal in California, but addicts were stigmatized by society and often targeted by law enforcement. The origin of the use having come from China led to it often being used as racist shorthand when referring to someone from China or used as a pretext for raiding Chinese businesses. The regular inclusion of opiates in several tonics and patent medicines at the time served to introduce many to the drug, leading to addiction. It was opium and revenge that may have led several in the Sacramento Gang into harm's way.

10

THE BATTLE OF MANZANITA HILL

There they are boys!
—*Alonzo T. Bell, Company H, Second Infantry, with the National Guard*

July 31, 1903

The Manzanita Gang headed south toward Lotus. Reports mention several encounters over the following days between travelers on the road and one or several members of this group, which likely included Wood, Theron, Miller, Eldridge and Murphy.

Over the next few days, encounters happened on the roads and near the Jurgens home in Weber Creek. Anna Jurgens maintained a home with several children (perhaps grown by this time) and had been in the area for quite a long time, having arrived in 1854. Since their arrival in California from the island of Heligoland, Denmark, the Jurgens had been part of the community, having owned a store, a vineyard and a mine. There are reports of the group of five staying here for several days and being civil guests of the Jurgens, with one account even including the playing of the family piano by one of the convicts.[77] At Weber Creek is a trestle crossing the creek and canyon that opened in 1903.

A few miles farther south from Weber Creek, the Grand Victory mine had been started in 1857 and had grown to one of the largest producers of gold ore in the Mother Lode region.

The gold was extracted using huge machines called stamps, which have a heavy weight that is dropped on or pushed onto pieces of ore to crush it into smaller pieces so gold can be found. Each stamp can weigh 750 pounds. Stamps are usually attached to each other in sets attached to a pulley or drive shaft. The stamps are lifted and dropped forty to fifty times per minute, crushing rock each time. With forty stamps running for years, millions of tons of rock had been removed from the area around the Grand Victory Mine.

The scale of the mining operation left the area transformed from rolling foothills that included gentle valleys with a creek running through to broken terrain with enormous piles of crushed ore and rock scattered about. The piles became softened by rain and snow from sharp peaks to irregular mounds with scrub brush and thick growths of manzanita, which made them almost impenetrable and created a maze among the bushes and remnants of the bounty pulled from the soil.

The "Gold Country" in California is a relatively small area, and from the Jurgens homestead near Pilot Hill and present-day Rescue, California, to the Grand Victory mine is about twenty miles directly but likely took a few more miles, as roads had to bend around river crossings for the South Fork American River, as well as several valleys, while also going up nearly one thousand feet in elevation.

When the gang reached the outskirts of the Grand Victory Mine, it must have looked like outlaw heaven with ditches, mounds, holes and piles and piles of rock, dirt and machinery to hide in, around and behind.

The scarred landscape had not grown back to its original state, but at least one native plant had made a comeback: "Arctostaphylos manzanita is a tall, beautiful species of manzanita with an often dramatic and winding branch structure. It has the common names of Whiteleaf Manzanita and Common Manzanita. It is native to California, where it can be found primarily in the North Coast Range, and in the northern and central Sierra Nevada foothills. The leaves are bright shiny green, wedge-shaped and pointed. The small white flowers are urn shaped. The fruits are berries that are white when new and turn red brown as the summer wears on. The bark on the long, crooked branches is reddish, making the shrub easily identifiable as a manzanita. It grows into a twisted tree about fifteen feet tall."[78]

Most importantly for the men on the run, the shrub grew thick around the remnants of the Grand Victory Mine and gave the area its name, Manzanita Hill.

The same day desperate men were digging in among the manzanita, Sheriff Keena of Placer County was losing faith after several days of his posse not seeing the fugitives, and said, "I believe the convicts have separated, and skipped out." He was half right. They had separated but hadn't left just yet. But given the sentiments of the sheriff, several of the posses, including Company H from Placerville, went home.

August 1, 1903

In the early morning hours of August 1, the piano-playing convicts left the Jurgens and headed farther south on Pleasant Valley Road, where they had breakfast at the home of Andrew Kamenzind. It's not clear if they knew Kamenzind or just dropped into his cabin at the headwaters of Martinez Creek. From there, the group continued on, and at about 10:00 a.m. they crossed a road in front of young Fred Twitchell, who was picking apples in his grandfather's orchard. When Fred saw five men, one quite heavyset, all with short hair and no beards and four of them carrying rifles, he knew something wasn't right. They were seemingly trying to cross the road while leaving as few tracks as possible.

Fred went to tell his grandfather what he had seen, and his grandfather, who was county supervisor W.W. Hoyt, thought it was interesting enough that he flagged down Elizabeth "Lizzie" Cosens, wife of George F. Cosens, who was on her way to Placerville in her wagon and asked her to let them know in town that the escapees may be in the area.

While Lizzie was in Placerville, passing on what she'd been told by Supervisor Hoyt, word also came in from Andrew Kamenzind about his breakfast visitors. Then a third message came to town from David Gipe, who was the caretaker at the Grand Victory Mine. He said he had been visited earlier in the day by two men who bought supplies from him, including eggs, matches, bread and salt, and that he'd seen three others standing off in the distance.

All the sightings were enough to persuade Sheriff Bosquit to make a midday phone call to C.A. Swisler, an attorney in Placerville and captain of Company H, Second Infantry, with the National Guard. The sheriff relayed the stories of the multiple reports on the escaped convicts in the area and asked if Swisler could have some of the members of Company H go out as a posse. Swisler had just the night before relieved the company from field service but, on further pressure from the sheriff, agreed to try to rally at least some of the company.

Downtown Placerville, 1866. *Courtesy of Library of Congress.*

Swisler then made calls to Thomas Smith, a lieutenant in Company H, and William C. "Bill" Burgess, another member of the company. After finishing his lunch, Swisler headed to downtown Placerville and, at the foot of Coloma Street where it met Main Street, ran into Festus and Will Rutherford, two brothers and members of Company H, who were hitching a ride home on a wagon that had been used by the company for commissary when they were out in the field. Or at least they had thought they would be heading home—they first ran into Dallas Bosquit, son of the sheriff, and then Captain Swisler.

According to the elder Rutherford,

> *Captain Swisler hailed us and came down and asked us if we had heard the report, and I said that we had heard the rumor and he said the sheriff had telephoned him that there had been five men seen near Hoyt's place and*

wanted to know if he could detail eight men or about eight men to go out and investigate and wanted to know if could go and I told him that I had seen Sheriff Bosquit and told him I could not go because I thought we were still under orders, and he said "No, you are mistaken, you were dismissed last night," and I said well it was simply a misunderstanding and if that was the case I was ready to go volunteer to go as a posse, and he said he would be glad if I would volunteer to with the other scouts and I said all right and my brother also stated his willingness to go.

The brothers then joined others, including Lieutenant Smith, Bill Burgess, Alonzo T. Bell, Henry Walters, A.W. Gill and Griffith Jones, who had been with the company during their recent field deployment.

The posse in their wagons made a few stops on the way to the Grand Victory to gather more information before coming to the boardinghouse at the mine. Gill knew the area well, as five years prior he had worked at the mine and lived on that hill for two years. At the boardinghouse, they spoke with David Gipe, who explained the men had been there and pointed out the direction they'd headed when they left.

After the trip from Placerville—which was mostly downhill—and likely in a bit of a hurry, the posse went into the area of the mine on foot at about 4:30 p.m. and formed a line to begin a search of the area. The terrain was broken, rough and covered with brush and thickets, which provided cover for desperate men as well as native wildlife like the northern Pacific rattlesnake, which grows four to six feet long and is well established in this area, accounting for several deaths from their venom over the years. The likelihood of an encounter, the terrain and the possibility of deadly reptiles may have moved the group to approach the area with caution.

According to Gill, they followed Gipe's directions and almost immediately found the tracks of two men. They followed the trail across a ravine and onto a dirt road and then up a steep incline through the brush.

In the group were several experienced trackers, and they identified five distinct tracks, with four of them described by Bill Burgess:

One of them was a very short track that looked almost like a boy's shoe, it was rather broad and a full round toe. It had nails along around the outer edges and in the middle or sole there was not as many nails as there was around the outer edges, that seemed to be worn or gone or something. That was about a number six or six and a half shoe. It was a remarkably short foot for a man, it was what you might call a stubby foot. Then there was another track of exactly the same style shoe but slightly larger and had nails in it and one half of one of the heels was gone. The same style of shoe as the very short shoe, the first track described and one half of one of the heels was gone, it looked from the impression as the heel might have been split lengthwise. There was another track that had a smooth sole, a remarkably long shoe, it must have been a ten or eleven, it was a very long shoe.... The fourth one I remember was somewhere about a seven or perhaps a seven and a half. It was a neat, very neat smooth sole, a sort of half square toe, and looked something like the sole of a half dress shoe, the sides were not parallel they came towards a point and instead of making a pointed shoe they turned off short and made a sort of a half square toe, it was a smooth sole.

Moving carefully, Bell climbed atop a log, where he spied several men in a thicket just fifteen feet away, and he whistled and cried out, "There they are boys!"

The first shot came down the hill at the posse, and everyone dropped. Burgess got up and took a shot at the smoke he saw coming from the manzanita. After his shot, Will Rutherford asked if Burgess had seen anyone, and Burgess responded, "No, there are two lines of smoke, one in this direction to the right and one on the side right in there. Look out, our boys are up there somewhere, be careful you don't hit them."

Gill added, "Here they are," and moved his rifle to fire, but before he could, he was hit in the chest by a shot. He fell, hit the log and rolled over; then he saw Jones with a bullet hole in his face and lying on top of his gun. Festus Rutherford was also on the ground on his right side with his rifle lying in a manzanita bush, having fallen after he got off two or three shots.

Gill crawled through the brush as the bullets kept flying from both sides and got progressively weaker from loss of blood.

As the gunfire began to slow, Gill heard Burgess down below yell up, "Where are they?"

Gill called back, "You had better keep down, they have killed two of the boys and I am down."

Will Rutherford and Burgess pressed up the hill; they saw brush move and heard what sounded like reloading of a magazine. Burgess fired into the brush, and they kept moving until they reached a wire fence at the top of the hill. Rutherford wanted to head back down and told Burgess, "I am afraid they have killed my brother." Burgess suggested they needed to keep moving—otherwise, they were going to end up the same way.

Gill's voice caught the attention of one of the escapees, and a face popped up in the brush ahead of him. He thought it might have been Murphy, and he got off three shots but wasn't sure if any found their mark. After this exchange, Gill decided he'd had enough and crawled along the log until he was over the crest of the hill, where he could then walk down and hopefully find some help. He got down to the boardinghouse, where he didn't find anyone, and tried walking along the road to go to another cabin but ran out of energy and lay down in the road.

As Gill lay in the road with a bullet that came in through his chest and then stopped at the skin of his back, Festus Rutherford, just two months short of his nineteenth birthday, and Griffith Jones, aged twenty-four, both lay dead in the manzanita brush. The mortal wounds for the almost nineteen-year-old were from at least two bullets that tore through his body. The first bullet entered on his right-hand side, between his second and third rib, and went all the way through his body, passing right by his heart, before exiting on the left side between his fourth and fifth rib, counting from above. A second bullet entered his left arm about twelve inches below his shoulder and then broke up into many pieces.

Under cover fire, the rest of the posse retreated to the base of the hill and the safety of the cover of their wagons.

Lieutenant Smith directed riders back to town for reinforcements and hunkered down to wait, as they figured there was no way off the hill for the desperados.

The frontier justice ethos that had led locals to name the town Hangtown, the seat of El Dorado County, also led many to want to help bring the escapees to justice, so the lawful posses and militias were joined by many others who wanted to help—or maybe just be part of something exciting.

The Hangtown name had been well earned by 1854, when it was renamed Placerville, which in 1903 had a population of nearly two thousand, about equal to its elevation above sea level on the western slopes of the Sierra Nevada, compared to about thirty thousand in Sacramento about forty miles west and downhill. Not long after the first gold seekers came to the area, following the discovery at Sutter's Mill, they were closely followed by those looking to find their gold in the pans and pockets of others rather than in the rivers, streams and mountainsides where it could be found. In 1849, one of these thieves was caught by a group that became a mob, and there was a call of "Hang him," which was promptly accomplished with a rope and a nearby tree in Elstner's Hay Yard. That was the first of several hangings of suspected thieves from the same tree in the Hay Yard, the stump of which can now be found almost 150 years later in the basement of a building in downtown Placerville called the "Hangman's Tree." The name of Old Hangtown became so synonymous with the town that it was on the town logo for many years, likely starting in the 1970s, before being removed in 2021.

Along with the militia was a posse led by Deputy John Bosquit, who was the son of Archie Bosquit, El Dorado County's sheriff. This group included deputies, guards and other assorted civilians.

With this group that eventually numbered nearly 150 arrived by 7:30 or 8:00 p.m., still a bit before sunset, the hill was surrounded, or so they thought, with men every twelve paces or so. With the area seemingly secured, the decision was made to wait the situation out overnight.

Given this was a mixed group holding siege to the hill, not all present were members of the militia and might not have followed those orders. Around 2:00 a.m., Louis Phillip Stringer, or Will, of Ringgold, a small community in the area—not a member of the militia but a volunteer posse guard—was moving through the brush when he was challenged by William Blake and Private Westlake, who were on guard. Blake called out to Stringer to identify himself, and when he didn't receive a reply, he opened fire. Will Stringer was deaf, so he wouldn't have heard the challenge, and he became the third to die on Manzanita Hill when he was hit by at least two shots, to the back and to the wrist.

On August 2, the sun came up over the Sierra Nevada just after 5:00 a.m., and the pursuers had had enough. They prepared themselves for the next assault but decided to bring in another reinforcement, fire. California, and especially its foothills, burn easily, and before the arrival of hordes of gold seekers, millions of acres burned naturally each year. By 1903, the fear of fire and historic conflagrations like the Peshtigo Fire, which burned more than two thousand square miles in Wisconsin in 1871, had led to forest policies that discouraged the traditional use of fire. This perhaps led to the thickening of the thickets of scrub brush, which made searching difficult.

By 10:30 a.m., the hill had burned over, and the group had completed their search. Their circling of the hill with a man every twelve feet had apparently not been enough, as all they found was "three hats, three vests, a can of water, some rounds of ammunition, and two revolvers. A pair of field glasses, stolen by Convict Wood from the store at Pilot Hill, was also picked up."[79]

After nearly twenty hours, the Battle of Manzanita Hill was over with nothing to show for it—except for the dead bodies of three local men—and no idea how many fugitives were even there and, most importantly, where they went.

Will Rutherford picked up his brother's lifeless body, put it on his back and carried it down the hill. John Copeland of Placerville picked up the feet of Griffith Jones and, with the help of two others, brought the bodies down the hill and past the boardinghouse, where they were laid out before transport back to Placerville.

On August 1, the Battle of Manzanita Hill was one of the last times a posse rode out in California after fugitives. That same day, another piece of western lore died as well when Calamity Jane died 1,200 miles east in Terry, South Dakota.

Company H, while unsuccessful in capturing the fugitives, was more successful with having its expenses reimbursed, receiving $498.40 from the State of California on March 31, 1905, for "amount due officers and enlisted men of Company H, Second Infantry Regiment, National Guard of California, who performed active service in pursuit of escaped convicts from Folsom Prison, California from July 27, 1903 to July 31, 1903, both inclusive, pursuant to orders of the Governor, said amount being for pay as per copy of pay roll hereto attached."[80]

August 2, 1903

The first report of importance to reach the prison today, relating to the hunt for the slayers of the militiamen at the Grand Victory Mine last Saturday evening came from Sheriff Bosquit.

He sent a message stating that last night four men supposed to be part of the five engaged in the fight last Saturday night called at the cabin of a man named Eades, four miles southwest of Fair Play, near the Consumnes river at 9 o'clock last night, and robbed his cabin of all the provisions it contained.

After the men had left, Eades notified Sheriff Norman of Amador County, which is just south of El Dorado County, and a posse of twelve or fifteen men was organized at once and started for the locality of Fair Play. Bosquit reports he has sent a posse to head the suspects off. The community of Fair Play is about 10–15 miles south of the Grand Victory Mine.

The fact that only four men called at Eades' cabin leads Bosquit to believe that one of the convicts engaged in last Saturday evening's battle at

Grand Victory Mine, was either killed by the pursuers, or so badly wounded that he was shot by his comrades or killed himself.

Bosquit states that he has been informed that about an hour after the fight a shot was heard in the direction which the convicts took, and it is supposed to have been the one which undoubtedly ended the existence of one of the three criminals.[81]

AUGUST 3, 1903

Following the Battle of Manzanita Hill—and the realization that several members of the California National Guard had died without any resulting captures—there was greater interest at the state level, and Governor George Pardee increased the award for the arrest of each inmate to $500, a significant increase from the $100 for each offered prior.

Whereas, On the 27th day of July, A.D., 1903 Frank Miller, No 5358, Henry Eldridge, No 5345, Joseph Theron, No 4419, Fred Howard, no 4228, John H. Wood, No 5090, Edward Davis, No 5096, Joseph Murphy, No 5324, A. Seavis, No 4810, James Roberts, No 5315, R.M. Gordon, No 4748, Ray Fahey, No 4967, and Frank Case, No 5099, convicts confined in the State Prison at Folsom, Sacramento County, California, escaped therefrom, after killing Guard William L. Cotter, and severely wounding two others; and whereas since their escape a party of said convicts, on the 1st day of August, 1903, killed William Griffin Jones and J.F. Rutherford, both members of a pursuing posse; Now, Therefore, I, GEORGE C. PARDEE, Governor of the State of California, by virtue of the authority in vested by the Constitution and the laws of said State, revoking the proclamation of reward of $100 issued July 27th, A.D. 1903, do hereby offer a reward of (Five Hundred Dollars) for the arrest of each of the said escaped convicts, payable upon his being delivered alive to the Warden of the State Prison at Folsom, or if during an attempt to arrest any of the said convicts he shall make such resistance as to endanger the persons or lives of his pursuers, and shall in consequence thereof be killed, said reward shall be payable to the person or persons who may have killed him, upon proof of said convict's death and the circumstances attending it.

IN WITNESS WHEREOF, I have hereunto set my hand and caused the Great Seal of State to be hereunto affixed, this 3d day of August, A.D. 1903.

George C. Pardee
Governor

Attest:

C.P. Curry, Secretary of State

AUGUST 8, 1903

Popular culture began to build around what was being called the "Manzanita Gang" and their miraculous escape, with multiple letters, editorials and even advertisements becoming part of the story.

"The Fair, W.H. Sumner proprietor" in Placerville advertised in the *Mountain Democrat* (which is still published and touts itself as California's oldest newspaper, founded in 1851): "The Bandits May Escape—You will not be wise however if you allow these prices to escape you," with specials on items ranging from coffee and tea to axle grease, tapioca and walnuts.

The story reached well beyond California, as two criminals in Clark, Missouri, robbed a clothing store and claimed to "be members of the gang of convicts that escaped from the Folsom Penitentiary in California."[82] Following their robbery, the criminals took over the farm of Edward Morton and at gunpoint "compelling Mrs. Morton to prepare three square meals for them."

Food was at the forefront of the minds of the escapees, and before they left, they again had "Mrs. Morton prepare a luncheon for them, repeatedly threatening the Mortons with death if they attempted to put the officers on their track. The Mortons were so terrified that they said nothing about their experience until long after their unwelcome visitors had departed."

While it was never confirmed anyone from this group made their way to Missouri, there were similarities to when in their first hours of freedom the Folsom escapees took over the Pilot Hill Hotel.

Back in California, food was also part of the story, as it was reported the Manzanita Gang had stopped for breakfast near Dogtown, present-day Caldor, a company town named for the California Door Company, the ignition point for the Caldor Fire of 2021, and

> *breakfasted at the cabin of one Richardson, a sheep herder on the ranch of Louis Meiss situated a few miles east of the Capp orchard, and about four miles north of Dogtown where Sheriff Norman's posses were located yesterday afternoon.*
>
> *Richardson rode to Grizzly Flat soon after the departure of the convicts and telephoned the news of the occurrence to Sheriff Bosquit at this place. Sheriff Bosquit took immediate action and sent a message to intercept the men who left there last night with bloodhounds, dogs to track the convicts by scent, to get them to proceed with great speed to Richardson's cabin, there to take the trail of the convicts.*
>
> *Sheriff Bosquit received word from Grizzly Flat this evening that the dogs and men passed through that place this afternoon on the way to Richardson's. D.E. Ferrell, who owns and manages the bloodhounds, expects to take up the scent before sundown and track the convicts as far as possible during the night. Bosquit's posse, which left here Monday night, is expected to be on the scene within a few hours.*
>
> *Sheriff Bosquit telephoned to the office of Sheriff Norman at Jackson, Amador County, to have a messenger dispatched from that place to Dogtown, and to inform Sheriff Norman and his posse of fifteen men of the developments this morning.*[83]

The posse was led by Deputy Gilbert Cook, who in 1906 would succeed Bosquit as El Dorado County sheriff. This group covered ground from Manzanita Hill up the Sierra Nevada to the Nevada state line, which is more than sixty miles away, and back over seventeen days. During this search over extremely rough terrain, the elevation climbed from less than two thousand feet at Placerville to more than seven thousand near Kirkwood, which is just over fifty miles up the hill. Cook was reelected as sheriff, running unopposed in 1910, before taking his own life in 1912 due to failing health following several heart attacks and a constitution that it was said never recovered after the brutal search of more than two weeks for the Manzanita Gang.

Also on August 8, it was reported that while there was a lot of action for the escapees, it was also dangerous for those left behind, especially for William Grider, who had tried to raise an alarm about the escape while it was still in the planning stages.

Two attempts to murder Convict William Grider have been made by prisoners at Folsom in retaliation for his having attempted to give information in advance of the recent prison break. Grider was a cellmate of Harry Eldridge, one of the convicts who escaped.

Grider informed a trusty named Barton that a break was to be made and asked him to report it to the officers. Barton paid no attention to Grider's statement beyond telling him to report the matter to Turnkey P.J. Cochrane. Grider told Barton that if he spoke to Cochrane, Eldridge would kill him. At this juncture, Eldridge came up to Grider and asked what he had said to Barton. Grider replied that he had said something about not going to work that day. Eldridge kept at Grider's side until the men were let out for their work and the latter had no chance to communicate the information he had.

Eldridge had told Grider the previous evening of the plan to escape, but Grider refused to join in the break. Eldridge pulled a knife on Grider in their cell and threatened to kill him if he ever told anybody about the then postponed break.

Last Thursday evening Grider was assaulted by Convict George Donnelly and a fierce fight followed. Donnelly was finally overpowered by the prison guards and sent to the dungeon.

Yesterday morning about a dozen convicts assaulted Grider, beating him over the head with the iron buckets with which all the cells are furnished. Grider's assailants were beaten off by the guards and locked up.[84]

11

ON THE RUN IN THE SIERRA NEVADA

August 4, 1903

Just three days after heading out with a posse of fellow guardsmen, Festus Rutherford and Will Jones were buried with full military honors on a hot Tuesday with the temperature reaching ninety-five degrees Fahrenheit in their hometown of Placerville.

The Union Cemetery in Placerville, California, was well established, having been founded more than thirty years prior by many local fraternal organizations such as "the F. & A. Masons, the Independent Order of Odd Fellows, the Independent Order of Red Men, and the California Grove of United Ancient Order of Druids."[85] Beyond the dedicated areas for members of these groups to lie forever are areas for those who died in service of the United States.

The headstones are next to each other and simply designed with "J.F. Rutherford," and "W.G. Jones" inscribed at the top of each, with a separate monument from their National Guard company.

While Rutherford and Jones were being laid to rest, about forty miles away in Sacramento, there was an alleged sighting of Albert Seavis reported in the *Daily Morning Union* of Grass Valley on August 6, 1903 (warning for racist stereotypes in the following depiction as reported).

Sheriff Reese and a number of deputies and citizens were sitting in the front office of the sheriff at a late hour the other night at a late hour the other night when the outside door was softly opened, and a negro youth, dusty and travel worn, with a bandana handkerchief around his neck appeared at the guard rail. All in the room turned instantly and fastened their gaze on the young negro. A thought which flashed through the minds of many present was given expression by Sheriff Reese, when he demanded:

"Good heavens! Are you Seavis?"

The young man's mouth widened to an extent that would admit a quarter section of watermelon.

"Me Seavis? Golly no," he said. "But I tell you boys, I look pretty much like him, dat's a fact, sure. Dey told me over on de Grant. I'd better keep my eyes peeled along de road or I'd get shot."

It developed that the young man had trudged in from Rancho del Paso to pay a visit to a horseman who had been jailed for some minor offense. It was too late to admit visitors to the jail, and the negro departed, not, however, until Sheriff Reese eyed him carefully again, and said in a tone that was not at all jocular: "Say, young man, you keep away from El Dorado. Do you hear?"[86]

August 23, 1903

Following the Battle of Manzanita Hill, much of the group that escaped from the Company H Posse may have first headed south before going east up the Sierra Nevada. The Manzanita Gang traced in reverse the rough route the ill-fated Donner Party had been trying to complete just over fifty years earlier, but while the Donner Party was trying to get to California for opportunity, these men were running for their lives away from the Golden State. From the foothills, the elevation increases rapidly, going from one thousand to six thousand feet within ninety miles. Along with the steep incline, the terrain is riven with deep valleys carved by millions of years of runoff from melting snows that drive the rapids of the American and Bear Rivers. The valley walls and rises are made of granite formed millions of years earlier when the Farallon Plate subducted below the North American Plate, creating a hard, dynamic and unforgiving landscape.

It's anywhere from 120 to 150 miles to Reno, Nevada, from the foot of Manzanita Hill, and with the rugged terrain, it's not easy traveling. When the Donner Party came through from east to west, they followed a trail that would have gone through the present-day town of Truckee, which didn't exist when they came through. By 1900, Truckee had around 4,500 residents and was an important rail stop on the transcontinental railroad. Its status as a growing railroad town also led to several saloons, as well as a culture used to seeing people come in and out of town.

The Truckee River is the only outlet from Lake Tahoe, the largest alpine lake in North America, and runs from the lake northeast to the town of Truckee and then east through Reno before it empties into Pyramid Lake, about thirty-five miles northeast of Reno. The route of the Truckee River was also followed by Wood, Murphy, Theron and Miller, who were spotted in Tahoe eating. They had likely traveled together since Manzanita Hill, although Murphy later said he met up with Miller at Lake Tahoe. Harry Eldridge may have left Manzanita Hill with the group, but by the time they got to Tahoe, he was gone.

From Tahoe, the group went through Truckee and may have taken the Lake Tahoe Transportation Company train, which began service in 1899 and ran from the lake to Truckee along the river. They then split up again: Murphy and Miller went to Reno, and Wood and Theron departed for Carson City.

> *At about 5:00 p.m. the two Reno-bound convicts boarded a train at Steamboat Springs south of Reno near the Geiger Grade, but their luck was beginning to run out. They had been spotted, and a phone call alerted Reno sheriff's deputies that the two men were headed their way, and to be on the lookout for the armed convicts.*[87]

By 8:00 p.m., there was another call letting deputies know the escapees were on South Virginia Street near the Southside Tavern. Where the Truckee River runs through Reno, there has been a bridge as long as there has been a Reno. Virginia Street runs across the Truckee River with what was then called the Iron Bridge. The Iron Bridge was built in 1877 for $16,000 and was a state-of-the-art iron bowstring arch truss that included separate spaces to keep pedestrians away from buggies and carriages. The Iron Bridge would stand until 1905, when it was replaced by a reinforced concrete bridge that became known as "Wedding Ring Bridge." During Reno's heyday as a divorce capitol, the recently divorced would walk out of the courthouse and onto the bridge to fling the rings signifying their now defunct marriages into the swirling waters of the river.

View of Virginia Street iron bridge over the Truckee River, downtown Reno. Caption on image: "Bridge over the Truckee River on Virginia Street, sometimes known as the Old Iron Bridge." *Courtesy of UNR Online digital Collection.*

At ten o'clock on that Sunday night, there were no celebratory divorcees at midspan but Deputies Sharkey and Maxwell, who were there under orders from Sheriff Hayes, along with Dwight Jones, a local man, and reporter Gerald F. Bacon of the *Reno Gazette*. Miller and Murphy had been walking quickly, as they thought they had been spotted on Mill Street but slowed their pace as they saw the small group on the bridge so they didn't seem too conspicuous. The attempts at subterfuge were futile, as Maxwell made the identification and said, "We have got our men." He and Sharkey commanded the two men to stop. Maxwell pulled his revolver to cover the escapees as they met on the bridge; Murphy was undeterred and tried to reach for his gun, which he had hidden "inside of my coverall, before I came upon the street, to get it out of sight." He had hidden it too well, as he didn't get to it before Maxwell disarmed him and said, "Don't do that."

Miller was on the far side of Murphy and took advantage of the cover provided by his compatriot to take his leave from the situation and leaped over the railing of the bridge into the willows and underbrush eight feet below on the riverbank. He may have fired two shots and said, "Take that," as he descended into the darkness. As he jumped, Sharkey fired, and then Maxwell followed with two more shots at Miller.

Sharkey then deputized Jones right there on the bridge and told Maxwell to hold onto Murphy, and he and Jones went over the railing into the darkness after Miller.

Sharkey led the way in the chase, trying to see by lighting matches, and Jones followed him carrying Sharkey's gun. Gunshots rang out of the darkness near Jones, but they may have been fired by another deputy who was converging from around a nearby building.

When the smoke cleared, Murphy was in custody and Miller was gone. No one had seen what happened to Miller, but Murphy thought he'd been hit by at least one shot, "When Maxwell opened up, I thought the first shot was at me and told him then he was a bad shot, but I think his second bullet hit Miller. It was all done so quick."

Some later reports said Miller had gone into the water of the Truckee River and, after submerging, never came up. Maybe he was staying underwater while he moved downstream and using the water to hide and protect himself.

12

CAPTURES

August 5, 1903

Eleven miles west of Sacramento was the village of Davisville (shortened to Davis in 1907), home to a few hundred settlers and the ancestral home of the Puttoy tribe of the Patwin, whose population had severely declined due to an epidemic seventy years earlier. In 1903, the residents were primarily involved in agriculture with farms and orchards in the fertile valley land.

Davisville was along Putah Creek, which flows east from the Mayacamas Mountains in the California Coast Range and then nearly sixty miles until it reaches the Sacramento River, having been diverted around the town with a channel in the 1870s to address frequent flooding. The name derived from what Spanish settlers had called the local tribe, according to local lore,[88] and was then modified, as it may have had negative connotations.

A railroad line ran from Sacramento to Davisville on the way to San Francisco, and James Roberts followed the tracks with the goal of catching a train and a ship out of the harbor in the bay. Someone in Sacramento tipped off the sheriff's office in Sacramento that Roberts and Fred Howard were headed this direction, and a posse led by Undersheriff Brown and Deputy Sheriff Griffin, along with Deputies Edward Reese, Jack Hunter and George Winterbrock from Sacramento and Officers Hainlino and

Johnson from Davisville, attempted to intercept them. Deputy Reese was one of six children of Sacramento sheriff David Reese, aged fifty-two at the time, who was elected sheriff in 1902 after running as an independent and serving two terms as an undersheriff. He had come to California as a child with his family after emigrating from Wales at age five. They lived in New Orleans, Kansas City and Utah before coming to California by ox team in the 1860s.

Reports at the time attributed the information leading to Robert's capture to an ex-convict named Newman, who had been followed to an opium den[89] by deputies and who then gave up their intended location.

The posse broke into two groups to search the area around Putah Creek and had no luck until they came upon a hobo camp that included a Folsom prison convict who had been recently released and knew both Roberts and Howard. While he said he had not seen them, suspicions were raised enough that the search persisted and expanded into a nearby area called Hamel Island. It was on the edge of Hamel Island just a few hundred yards from a railroad bridge that the posse found Roberts "lying under a tree, he had been asleep." He was wearing a "striped shirt, brown pantaloons, and a dark vest,"[90] and had with him a pair of tan shoes in addition to heavy leather shoes he was wearing.

With him was a .45-caliber revolver, but given he was asleep, he was awakened by the group and held up his hands when asked to and then submitted to handcuffs.

Roberts was concerned about the potential repercussions of his escape but not that he had done it. He held fast to the belief that he had been wrongly imprisoned and said he was "sent to prison on the testimony of a deserter and that he was innocent of the crime of which he was convicted."

That was overshadowed by his bravado in perhaps facing the gallows for his escape. He said a man has only one time to die but stated, "You can't hold me for murder....Howard and I cleared away from the bunch before the fight at the Grand Victory Mine, where the militiamen were killed."

Whether or not he would be held accountable for crimes committed by other escapees, Roberts was in jeopardy for his role in the death of Guard William Cotter during the escape.

But where was Fred Howard? Roberts claimed he had left him in Sacramento after they disagreed on going into town to buy more opium. But there were eyewitness reports of two men fitting their description together in Chinatown the night before.

August 6, 1903

On May 19, 1903, President Theodore Roosevelt stopped in Auburn, California, about twenty miles northeast of Folsom Prison, at the train yard and gave remarks to an assembled crowd. He referred to the crowd, especially local miners, and said,

> *I have enjoyed to the full my visit to California. I have been astonished and delighted with your extraordinary success in so many different types of industries—mining, agriculture of so many kinds, manufacturing, your wonderful commerce. It is particularly a pleasure to be in a State already great, and yet with an infinitely greater future before it. But pleased though I am to see your abounding material prosperity, the products of your soil, the thing I am most pleased with is you yourselves, the men and women.*[91]

Roosevelt was on his way back to Washington, D.C., following a marathon trip of more than fourteen thousand miles that had led him to Yosemite Valley, where he camped with John Muir for three days, before catching a train on the eighteenth and began heading north.

Less than three months later, the Auburn depot was again in the center of the news as a conductor on a freight train reported that Albert Seavis might be on the train arriving from Roseville, about fifteen miles west, but more than a one thousand feet lower in elevation. Roseville was a busy shipping point with an active railroad junction while Auburn was more of a mining town, but both were in Placer County. Charles Keena, who had been born forty-three years earlier on a ranch at Rock Creek[92] just outside Auburn, was now sheriff.

Keena received word that someone matching Seavis's description had boarded overland freight train No. 241[93] at Newcastle, which is about eight miles north of Pilot Hill, the site of the gun battle of a week earlier, and four miles west of Auburn. While the distance from Pilot Hill is only eight miles, it crosses several steep valleys and at least one river.

The conductor, O.N. Nelson, saw a man climb onto a pusher engine when the train slowed at Newcastle, and then he told operator J.P. Schnitzius that he thought it was the escaped convict Seavis. Later, Seavis told reporters he had jumped the train one or two stops earlier, at Loomis or Penryn, but had just gotten down when the train stopped at Newcastle to look around when he was spotted.

At the time, there weren't many Black men in Placer County, which had a total population of just over fifteen thousand in 1900. More than one hundred years later, African Americans still make up less than one percent of the population of the county, so a Black man likely stood out, especially when there was an active manhunt.

When the train stopped in Auburn, the engineer, Ed Waters, approached the man, who was dressed in a light coat with dark trousers and had a felt hat pulled down over his face, and asked him where he was headed. The man responded, "Oh, I'm going harvesting over in Nevada."[94]

While this was happening, Schnitzius was contacting the dispatch yard in Sacramento, asking for permission to hold the train to give the sheriff time to check things out. It took more than twenty minutes for Sheriff Keena and Deputy Lee Coan to arrive.

When they entered the yard, they split up—each carrying a short-barreled repeating shotgun[95] loaded with buckshot—and took one side of the train where the fugitive was supposed to be hiding. They moved slowly along its length until one caught sight of Seavis and yelled at him to halt. Seavis wasn't ready to go just yet, so he turned and started to run, firing back as he made his escape.

He fired three shots from a revolver at Deputy Coan, all missing. Shooting a handgun at a moving target while running away makes it difficult to be effective, but a shotgun works very well, which is how Sheriff Keena responded. He knelt down and fired under the body of the freight car, hitting Seavis in the legs with enough shot for him to go down and be overtaken.

As Seavis dropped to the ground, he released his gun and yelled out, "Don't kill me, don't shoot," to which Keena replied with a command for him to put his hands up. Seavis emphatically complied, saying, "My hands are up, don't shoot!" He was taken into custody and held the rest of the night in jail in Auburn. The next morning, he was visited by Sacramento district attorney Arthur Seymour and Warren Doane, a court reporter, as well as reporter from the *San Francisco Call*, to whom he said, "I'm up against it, this is my last break, but I'll take my medicine like a man."

That day, he was transferred in handcuffs back to Folsom Prison in a surrey. He rode with Sheriff Keena and Sheriff Mansfield of San Mateo County and was quoted as saying, "I have had a good holiday." While Seavis was being freed from the irons, he added, "It was not so bad in the woods and was a change from this place."

Contemporary reports focus on the race of the one African American escapee and often separate his story from that of his Caucasian accomplices, for example: "The wives and children of the ranchers thinly settled districts of El Dorado County were delighted to hear of the capture of Seavis, for they felt a peculiar dread of the bloodthirsty black man, who was always ready to suggest murder."

An additional account of Seavis after his capture says he "expressed just one regret, and that was that he had not killed Deputy Sheriff Dependener who, he said, passed within three feet of him on a lonely trail below Newcastle the day before."[96]

Seavis was originally sent to Folsom Prison from Sacramento with a twenty-five-year sentence for burglary. His story didn't end when he was returned to Folsom following his capture. Ten years later, he was tried for the attempted murder of Albert Lopez, another inmate. It was alleged that Seavis assaulted Lopez with a prison-made knife, and given Seavis was already in custody with a life sentence, he was subject to a new law that had been passed following the 1903 escape: convicts serving a life sentence were exempt from all subsequent punishment short of death for murderous assault.

The judge in this trial, Joseph W. Hughes, had been appointed to the Superior Court of Sacramento[97] in 1899.

AUGUST 24, 1903

Monday is a great day to get a haircut or maybe a shave, and why should being on the run following breaking out of prison while sentenced to life imprisonment stop someone? It didn't stop John Wood, who came around the corner of Center Street in Reno at about 10:00 a.m. and into the barbershop run by Mr. Hanna.

He caught the eye of Constable Wilson, who thought he matched the description he'd read and the drawing he had seen of the escapees that were likely in the area. He was going to make the stop right then when he noticed a revolver under the man's coat, held in his belt. With that, Wilson decided discretion was the better part of valor and called for Chief of Police R.C. "Charles" Leeper, but not before he peeked into the window and caught the eye of B.W. DeHart, who was one of the barbers on duty inside.

Leeper had been chief for less than a year but was a well-established part of the community, having served a term in the Nevada state legislature from 1890 to 1892 and established a saddlery business before his appointment as the first police chief of Reno. As befitted his stature, he wore a cap with "CHIEF" embroidered on the front, above his walrus mustache, much like that worn by Mark Twain when he was living in the area forty years earlier.

Upon entering the shop, Wood removed his coat, with his gun in it, and then sat back in the chair. While he was getting settled, he saw the face looking through the window and asked his attendant, "Who is that fellow, I think I have seen him before." DeHart, who was catching on to what was transpiring, played it cool and said he "did not know although he had seen him very often around town." He knew who it was in his chair.

While Wood was getting settled, another man entered the shop and spoke with him openly before leaning into whisper in his ear. He then made an appointment for a later time and left the shop.

Together, Leeper and Wilson, out of breath, then entered the shop to find Wood in the barber chair with shaving cream on his face, a barber cape covering him, and likely a bit reclined. He was caught, and he knew it. When faced with two men with guns pointed at him, he put up no resistance as manacles were slapped onto his wrists.

The greeting from Leeper was "When did you come to town?" and Wood responded by saying he had recently arrived from Grass Valley and asked DeHart for his coat. DeHart motioned to the officers they should take a look at it, where they discovered a forty-five-caliber revolver.

With Wood safely manacled, Leeper and Wilson allowed DeHart to finish the shave before they transported him to the Washoe County Jail. While he was being moved to the lockup, a posse of more than one hundred men was combing the nearby train tracks, where it was thought Miller had escaped.

When Wood arrived at the jail, he asked Deputy Maxwell if he could be roomed with Murphy: "You should treat me well as long as I live. I know that hanging awaits me, and it cannot possibly do any harm to let me see Murphy."

While he may not have been able to see Murphy, he did later describe to Sheriff Leeper how they kept in touch at Folsom:

> He said it was a snap. There was a full-fledged mail route in operation between the cells. Wood said he possessed himself of a string and tossed it out into the corridor, whereby juggling with it for a few minutes, it came into Murphy's reach. Midway on the string a note would be tied. It was drawn in and a reply sent back. This was kept up day after day, the only interruption in the service being the approach of someone, when the string would be hastily drawn in.[98]

They had lots of time to catch up, as Washoe County authorities declined to release the prisoners to California until they received the stated reward. This ended up taking three weeks, giving the prisoners time to catch up, enjoy the food and even for Murphy to write an epic poem—or at least it's attributed to him—of his time. It was published in the *Daily Nevada State Journal* on August 30, 1903. Of his fare while in Washoe, Murphy said, "If the prison guards would treat us like Sharkey and Maxwell, the boys here, there would be fewer men in prison."

The Washoe County Jail

It was on the 23rd of August in the middle of the night,
While taking a walk through Reno we got into a fight,
The Sheriff and his deputies with their guns they did us assail,
And they gave us a hearty escort to the Washoe county jail.

They marched us up through Reno, and the people they did stare,
For they knew that we were convicts but little did we care
They marched us up to the sheriff's office, and searched us through
And devil a thing they found on us except "a gat" or two

They put us each in separate cells, upon the second floor
And when we wanted anything, we would rap upon the door
And when the Sheriff comes around shove out your little pail
And he will feed you bootleg coffee in the Washoe county jail

Monday and Tuesday, they give you Irish stew,
Wednesday and Thursday, beef and liver, too,
Friday and Saturday, "murphies" we pare without fingernails
For they won't give a "con" a knife and fork, in the Washoe county jail.

Every Sunday morning as they open your cell door,
You listen to a preacher until your ears are sore
And if we were outside our cells, the walls we'd try to scale
For they teach us bum religion in the Washoe county jail.

After three weeks, and affirmations from California officials that Washoe County would indeed be paid, the recaptured Wood and Murphy were escorted back to Folsom. Once the prisoners arrived, Washoe County and the State of Nevada continued to ask to be paid the promised rewards. As of October 6, 1903, the reward had not been paid, and local media was starting to get a bit testy, with the following appearing in the *Nevada State Journal*: "The officers who risked their lives in the capture of these outlaws were assured in answer to Governor Sparks' demand, that the reward would be paid immediately. Not a cent of the money has shown up and there is no indication that it will."

Beyond not paying the promised reward, California also paused in paying for expenses related to keeping the convicts since their capture and set a precedent for not paying this sort of bill received by the state related to the escape.

BACK BEHIND BARS

In every other capital case that has occurred this office has been approached by someone asking or suggesting clemency, but Murphy was apparently friendless.
—Secretary A.B. Nye

July 14, 1905

Convict Joseph Murphy, convicted of the murder of Guard William Cotter during the big break that occurred at the Folsom prison on July 27, 1903, paid the penalty of his crime on the gallows this morning at the institution.

Murphy spent a miserable night, as he was unable to sleep, except for about an hour before 4 o'clock, when he dropped off into an uneasy slumber and tossed and moaned. When his breakfast was brought to him, he ate sparingly, and it was only too evident that he was badly frightened.

When Warden Yell entered his cell and began to read the death warrant, Murphy said: "I don't want to hear that," and the further reading of the document was waived. After the usual preliminary preparations, Murphy left his cell with a guard on either side and walked upon the scaffold. He was deadly pale and refused to say anything. After the trap was sprung life was extinct in ten minutes.

"One of the most peculiar things about Murphy's case," said Secretary A.B. Nye at the Governor's office this morning, "is the fact that no application was made to the Governor by anyone to have his sentence

mitigated. In every other capital case that has occurred this office has been approached by someone asking or suggesting clemency, but Murphy was apparently friendless."

Murphy, with twelve other convicts, escaped from Folsom Prison [on] July 27, 1903, after an assault upon the prison officials, in which Guard W.L. Cotter was killed, Chief Turnkey P.J. Cochrane dangerously wounded, and the late Warden Thomas Wilkinson and Captain of the Guard R.J. Murphy and other officers captured and marched out of the prison grounds.

The convicts divided into two bands after the fight at Pilot Hill, in which one of their number, J.J. Allison, was killed. Murphy and John H. Wood, the leader of the band, worked their way to Reno, Nevada, where they were captured several weeks after the break. In their flight they had an encounter with a detachment of the militia company located at Placerville in which two members of Company H, Rutherford and Jones, were killed.

Wood and Murphy were returned to California for trial. Wood was tried in the Superior Court of this county, on a charge of murder, and despite the fact that he was serving a life sentence for robbery, the intelligent jury returned a verdict of murder in the second degree. No penalty within the law under this verdict could have added to Wood's sentence.

Afterward, Wood was tried in El Dorado County, convicted of the murder of the militiamen, and while awaiting execution at Folsom Prison, committed suicide by hanging.

Murphy was convicted of the murder of Guard Cotter by a jury in Superior Judge Hart's Court and sentenced to death. The Supreme Court, on appeal, sustained the judgment of the trial Court.

Harry Eldridge, another of the band of convicts, is awaiting execution, having been convicted of murder.[99]

In a twist of fate, the same month Joseph Murphy met his end on the gallows, the Iron Bridge in Reno where he was captured did as well, as it was dismantled in preparation for a new bridge, which still crosses the Truckee River today.

On July 18, the *Hanford Journal* published a poem[100] attributed to Murphy and submitted by an attorney, T.M. McNamara, who said he had several from the late felon. This was published, as was "The Washoe County Jail," the lament he penned after he was captured near Reno, Nevada. While his previous work focused on his accommodations and fare while in jail, this one focused on his time on the run.

It was just a few short days since from them we broke away;
Through the foothills we've been hiking night and day,
For it's up north we did go,
To the bank of Lake Tahoe,
And passed the sheriff's posse on the way, Oh!
Those posses showed cold feet,
For the cons they did not meet,
As along the route in ambush they all layed.
Well, we came along at last,
and the sheriff let us pass,
Then turning to his posse he did say:

CHORUS

The broke from the Folsom Prison
We won't catch them today;
We do not want a mix-up,
Are the words that he did say,
And to save our reputation,
So, of course, we did not see,
The cons, from Folsom Prison, far away.

March 31, 1904

The March 31, 1904 issue of the *Morning Oregonian* told of Harry Eldridge being taken by train back to California from Seattle after being captured there. Accompanying Eldridge was lieutenant of the guards at Folsom Prison P.J. Cochrane.

Eldridge asserted Cochrane would not be able to take him back successfully, but Cochrane—being a powerfully built six feet, two inches—took no chances and secured him for the trip with an Oregon Boot. The "boot" was a heavy leg shackle with a weight around the ankle supported by two bars that passed under the foot, making running, let alone walking, very difficult. The boot was patented in 1866 by Oregon State Penitentiary warden J.C. Gardner and was sometimes called the Gardner Shackle, as he developed this solution for how to secure inmates during the construction of a new prison. This method used a weight of up to twenty-eight pounds on the boot to slow down prisoners and was so heavy there were many issues with injuries to those forced to wear the boot for extended periods. The prevalence of injuries and changes to incarceration practices led to the Oregon Boot being phased out in the United States in the years following World War I. (It was reportedly used for the last time in 1939.)[101]

Cochrane may have been looking for additional ways to ensure compliance from the prisoner, as he was reported to have had two ribs removed because of injuries sustained in the attack by the prisoners during their escape.

Eldridge blamed his time in the boot and recapture on Charley O'Nell, a friend since childhood, who Eldridge said betrayed him. In the year between his escape and capture, he said he had worked many jobs, including briefly running a restaurant, claiming to be a farmhand and working as a hotel clerk in Terrace, Nevada (now Utah).

Terrace was a railroad town in the Great Salt Lake Desert founded by the Central Pacific Railroad on April 1, 1869, as a regional hub to service trains in a company-built roundhouse with sixteen stalls and a switchyard with eight tracks. The population peaked at about one thousand but was likely declining by the time of Eldridge's stay. In 1904, a change to the main train line to Ogden opened, leaving Terrace off the main line. The town shriveled until eventually the tracks were removed and Terrace became a ghost town.

DECEMBER 1, 1905

Harry Eldridge was executed at 10:00 a.m. by hanging at Folsom Prison for the murder of Guard W.L. Cotter. Impending death didn't make Eldridge any more genial, and he demanded the death warrant be read to him and refused consultation with the clergy for any final absolution. Until the end, he refused to take responsibility. Just before the trap door was released on the gallows, he was said to have blamed his situation on his trying to be free, rather than the murder he committed, and said he was being executed because he "tried to kick out of prison."

Capital punishment had been part of California almost as long as it had been a state, with legal executions authorized by 1851's Criminal Practices Act, although this was updated forty years later with an amendment from the legislature that moved executions from the county to the state level, stating "a judgment of death must be executed within the walls of one of the State Prisons designated by the Court by which judgment is rendered." Ironically the statute calls for executions to happen "within the walls" of one of the state prisons; at the time the statute was written, Folsom didn't have a wall.

Harry Eldridge is buried in the cemetery at Folsom Prison.

The first execution at Folsom Prison wasn't until 1895, and Eldridge was one of ninety-three, including two from the escape, who were executed on the banks of the American River. The last execution at Folsom Prison was in 1937, when Charles McGuire was executed for the murder of Sacramento candy shop owner Max Krall during an armed robbery.

August 18, 1908

Fred Howard was booked into San Quentin Prison on August 18, 1908, having been extradited from the Colorado Penitentiary in Canon City, where he had been prisoner no. 6863. His original mug shot from 1897, when he was sentenced to fifteen years for robbery, shows a young man of twenty-two with bright eyes and full dark hair with a mustache.

By the time he was brought back, he was a hardened man of thirty-four with one eye missing and a description of "top of left ear cauliflowered… small scar left side of forehead."[102] It was rumored he had lost his eye during the break, but there were no contemporaneous references to an injury.

He threw himself upon the mercy of the court, pleaded guilty to the killing of the guard during the break and asked for life imprisonment.

In 1923, he was transferred to Folsom Prison from San Quentin, ending up back where he had left during a bloody morning twenty years before. He died in Folsom Prison in 1941 at age sixty-six, having missed the hangman's noose, and although he was outside for five years, in the long run he didn't escape Folsom Prison.

September 16, 1911

On the morning of Tuesday, September 12, 1911, Eleanor Pryce was preparing for the day as a schoolteacher in Snowflake, Manitoba, Canada, where she taught the junior grades at Snowflake Consolidated School. Snowflake was a small farming town on the border with the United States, right across from Hannah, North Dakota.

Harry Eldridge, following his execution at Folsom Prison. *Courtesy of California State Archive.*

The day quickly changed when she was approached by a stranger and then abducted and taken on a harrowing journey into the woods, where she would be kept as captive for the next thirty hours. After she was released, or freed or escaped, she sounded the alarm, and a posse of two hundred locals went into the field looking for her assailant.

A few days later, Bill Miner was discovered hiding in a haystack on Tony Johnson's farm near Hannah, on the American side of the border, by a young boy who alerted authorities. They arrived by automobile and apprehended the suspect without a struggle.

Fearing the repercussions of the locals in Canada for the abduction of Miss Pryce, Miner confessed that he was really Edward Davis, convicted robber, and had been on the run since taking part in the bloody escape from Folsom years before.[103] He admitted he had been in Snowflake recently.

He had last been reported seen a week after the escape by Charles Darling in Natoma near Sacramento, when he and Ray Fahey were reported to have stolen a horse and cart from his stable. Following his capture, Davis said he had been in South America until three years prior.

Following the battle at Pilot Hill, Davis, along with Seavis, Roberts, Fahey, Case and Howard, split off and headed west toward Sacramento, while another group headed south and ended up in another battle at the Grand Victory Mine before heading east toward Reno.

NOVEMBER 22, 1913

James Roberts was paroled on November 22, 1913, and a week later he left Folsom Prison to begin a new life with a job in Sacramento as a laborer for Jeffrey Shops for a salary of fifty to fifty-five dollars per month.

His parole review included supportive statements from the district attorney of Sacramento and a former presiding judge, perhaps surprisingly, Judge E.C. Hart, who was the subject of so much ire from many of the escapees. Why were these people advocating for a twice-convicted felon who had been part of a bloody escape and convicted of second-degree murders as a result? He probably never should have been at Folsom.

Judge Hart, who played a pivotal role in the lives of so many of the prisoners, wrote on his behalf.

> Roberts was one of a number of prisoners who escaped from the prison in the big break of 1904 [sic], on which occasion a guard by the name of Cotter was killed by the escaping prisoners. My recollection is that the evidence disclosed that Roberts had nothing to do with the original conspiracy—that is that originally, he was not one of the conspirators—but that after the break was started in execution of the conspiracy, he joined in the crowd that escaped. He was regarded by the officers of our county jail, where he was confined for several months prior to his trial, as a weakling, mentally, and apparently harmless. This part was not brought out at the trial, and of course, could not properly have been shown in the absence of the interposition of the defense of mental irresponsibility.[104]

A separate letter from the district attorney of Sacramento County read

> I have interacted in the Roberts case, perhaps more than any living soul other than himself, and I feel confident that no better case for a parole exists. I learn from the prison officials that his record is par excellence. I have also discussed the matter with Hon. E.C. Hart, Justice of the Appellate Court of the Third District, with Mr. Arthur M. Seymour, being the Judge and the District Attorney respectively who participated in the trial of Roberts at the

time he was convicted, and I find them both willing to lend whatever aid they can towards assisting Roberts. I have also talked with Parole Officers and ascertain that they are much in favor of the granting of the parole. In fact, there seems to be no doubt whatever, but that Roberts is worthy of parole, and furthermore that the application should be granted. I feel certain that Roberts will live up to the rules and regulations of the board if a parole be granted to him, and am willing to undertake, if permitted, the guidance of and advice to Roberts, because I believe that much good can be done for the parole system in using Roberts as an example of what may be accomplished in this line.[105]

May 9, 1920

Being granted parole was not always easy, as there were often terms associated with being released. For example, on May 9, 1920, Albert Seavis was granted parole on the condition that he "obtain employment at sea." Over the next few years, several letters were exchanged seeking employment in this capacity, which means although he was granted parole almost seventeen years after the escape, he was still incarcerated. On May 15, 1921, the warden wrote a letter to the Pacific Steamship Company, saying that Albert Seavis had requested he write on his behalf regarding employment, as his parole was not active until he secured a job. The letter was straightforward in what it requested.

This man is a life-termer and has been granted a parole with the condition that he obtain employment at sea, and parole would be effective when satisfactory employment is submitted. In this regard, I will state that he is able-bodied, and is able to do any manual labor that you have to offer.

Included was a blank employment agreement. The response from the Pacific Steamship Company shows either the difficulty in securing employment for a felon or the theater that may have been going on to delay actual parole.

Regret having to advise that we have no employment to offer. Conditions are such that even if we were so inclined, we could not offer employment on board one of our vessels as the applicant would not be a Union man and you are no doubt well aware that Union men will not allow Non-Union men to work with them.

JULY 25, 1924

Seavis was eventually officially discharged from Folsom, and he left behind a poem that reflected his own attitudes as well as the societal racism that may have caused him to adopt the nickname of "Smokey" (which may have started as a slur).

TO THOSE I LEAVE BEHIND

As I leave these old grey walls behind,
And sail the Southern Sea –
I'll be talking often in mind,
Of You, who think of me

My misty meditations will –
No doubt, quite often span,
The far and distant land-scape
Putting some-one on the Pan,

For I know full well that many,
Will be indulging in the game –
At roasting poor old Smokey,
And maligning my good name.

If per-chance I've called the turn,
Then your pans will be all greasy;
(I expect my ears to burn)
So Please let me down, E-Z

Speaking here, as man to man
"What a helleva life 'twould be –
"If we had no one to Pan
"Or be-speak their faults quite free,"

So, Boys –Don't slight old Smokey,
If you do, My heart will break;
(I'd feel sad and rather chokey,)
Pan me Some, –For old time sake.

VIZ–
"Smokey this and Smokey that,"
"They've got him pinched for Mopery"
"They found a Sticker in his hat –"
"And now he's charged with Dopery."

Or—
In your latest News, –Please say –
"They took him out and Bumpt-um,"
"His carcass was found in Frisco Bay,"
"Where officer Whyte had Dumpt-um."

AND–
Next day, bring on some dope that's Straight,
"And whisper in a quivver [sic] –
"Smokey jumped the boat at Golden Gate,"
"And he's hiding across the river."

THEN–
With a knowing finger, point –
And say – "Don't you see him yonder?
He certainly loves this Folsom joint;
Then let the other fellow ponder.

NOW'S GOOD-BY,
Old Pale, I'm on my way
Where the winds are balmy and breezy;
GOOD LUCK to ALL,
And SAY will you please let me down E.Z.

Smokey[106]

EPILOGUE

SEPTEMBER 16, 1903

While there were still eight of the thirteen escapees at large, the State Board of Prison Directors was hard at work on a report on the escape itself. The scathing findings were submitted by Directors R.M. Fitzgerald, C.N. Felton, J.H. Wilkins and Don Ray on September 16, 1903, and called out the warden and guards for failing to do their duty, funding for prisons being inadequate and the congregant system itself for being antiquated and serving to make heroes out of convicts. The report seems to blame everyone but the convicts for the escape and spends a considerable amount of space lauding the trusties who did their jobs during the break while at the same time calling out the people of California who have a "sticky sentimentality," when concerned with prisoner safety.

At fault, according to the directors, were Warden Wilkinson and Captain Murphy for multiple lapses, including meeting each morning in the same location—where inmates knew they could be found—but also for not being willing to sacrifice their lives to prevent inmate escapes.

Yet the board is unanimously of the opinion that the officers and guards should have stopped this outbreak at all hazards. Unfortunate, as it may be to sacrifice a free man's life. In such a case, we believe that those who accept such positions, where duty sometimes makes it necessary to endanger their lives, this duty should be fearlessly performed. Your board is convinced that had the officers and guard who were attacked showed the same daring and nerve as the convicts who attacked them the convicts could never have left the prison grounds alive.

The report calls out three instances during the escape where Warden Wilkinson failed to be willing to sacrifice himself to prevent the escape, including when the gatekeeper, Dolan, was "instructed by the Warden and Captain Murphy to open the gate," and then when reaching the armory: "again Warden Wilkinson and Captain Murphy, as well as Lieutenant Kipp, ordered the guards not to fire, and the armory was surrendered to the convicts."

From the criticisms came the call for censure and veiled, or not so veiled, accusations of cowardice.

Your board is of the opinion that had either Warden Wilkinson or Captain Murphy refused to give the order to the guards not to fire when commanded to do so by the convicts, some of the officers and guards in the power of the convicts would have in all probability been severely injured, if not murdered, and in arriving at our conclusions we are not unmindful of this and fully realize the position the officers were placed in.

The report continues, "We do not charge the officers with cowardice, and believe that being completely surprised they acted as they did, not fully realizing the full sense of their duty until the matter was over and the convicts gone."

The guards are then called to task explicitly for allowing the escape and "so convinced is the board that it is the duty of all officers and guards to prevent the escape of convicts at every hazard that an order has been issued making it the imperative duty of all officers and guards to prevent convicts from escaping, whether they have free men in their charge or not, and when any such attempt is made by the convicts the guards must fire."

The board then criticized the use of "trusties," while following the criticism with laudatory descriptions for the actions of three of them during the break and going so far as to call for multiple pardons.

Whatever may be the wisdom of these appointments, on this occasion at least, every trusty who had it within his power rendered immediate and valuable service, both at the time of the break and to those who were so grievously injured.

We desire to call your attention especially to the case of Joseph Casey, a life termer received at the prison June 2, 1890, who had charge of the inner gate. When he saw the trouble in the yard, he immediately closed the gate and kept within the prison building 500 convicts, thus preventing what possibly might have been a general delivery.

The report continued with the behavior of John Martinez, who was serving a twenty-year sentence for rape and had been at Folsom since 1895. During the escape, Martinez rendered assistance to one of the injured guards, Chalmers, who was the gatekeeper, and finished his job by shutting the outer gate and putting the key to the gate into his own pocket.

Charles Abbott, who was serving a life sentence for murder and had been incarcerated for twenty years thus far, and O.C. Clark, serving a twenty-year sentence for forgery, were recommended for pardon for providing assistance to the gravely injured Cotter and Cochrane.

Lastly, the board recommended a pardon for William Grider, a convicted burglar from San Joaquin County who had just arrived in May and had been, until the escape, the cellmate of Harry Eldridge. Early on the morning of July 27, Grider notified a trusty (unnamed) about the planned escape, although there is no information about who the trusty was or why the trusty was unable to notify any guards or administration. Following the escape and subsequent disclosure about his attempts to stifle it, Grider was assaulted several times by other inmates before being locked in his cell for his own protection.

Following the criticism of the actions of guards and the congratulating of the trusties and inmates, the report bridges to criticism of the system as a whole and its funding while deflecting blame to others, including "misguided sentimentalists," saying, "Someday the people of California would learn the truth about the prisons of this state, and when understood, would respond as promptly and generously as they have to other departments of the government."

"It is a sufficiently difficult task to control the convicts of California under the system in vogue in this state, and which your board is convinced is a disgrace to the State, without the convicts feeling that the public at large sympathize with them and not with the officers of the law."

The congregate system, where "all are together in the same yard, young and old, bad and indifferent, is what we complain of and protest against."

This is related earlier, when the report states, "Many causes have led to the prison outbreak, not the least of which has been the record of convicts in other prisons who have become notorious because of their exploits in breaking jail and taking life after their escape and while being pursued."

The report then goes on to the lack of a wall:

Your Board has frequently called to the attention of the Legislature, the urgent need for a wall around Folsom Prison, but without avail. If a wall is not provided, sooner or later, life will be sacrificed in the effort to prevent other prison breaks. So convinced was your board of the necessity of a wall that, at a meeting of the board held prior to the recent outbreak, the warden was ordered to commence taking out granite to be used for this purpose, trusting the Legislature would make up any deficiencies that may thus be accrued and provide such appropriations as would enable the board to purchase the necessary cement and tools, and we hope our action will meet with your approval.

The report was signed by R. Fitzgerald (president) and members J. Wilkins, C. Fulton and D. Ray.

According to Michael D. Brown's *History of Folsom Prison*, "Neither the Governor, nor the Legislature was impressed with the report of the Prison Directors as it indirectly placed the responsibility for prison conditions on their shoulders, and implied that their failure to act upon requests for additional appropriations was a factor in the outbreak."[107]

Director Wilkins had more than a passing familiarity with the escape. According to an article titled "Wilkins Was a Hero" in the *Grass Valley and Nevada City Daily Morning Union* on July 30, 1903, he distinguished himself that day:

State Prison Director Wilkins was really the hero of the hour at the outbreak, though his part in the thrilling affair has just come to light.

Wilkins was visiting the prison as the guest of Warden Wilkinson. He was awakened early Monday morning by loud raps at his door and the cries of a servant that the warden and captain of the guard were being murdered at the captain's office by a gang of enraged convicts, armed with knives and razors.

Wilkins hastily donned his outer garments and seizing his revolver, lost no time in getting down the stone steps and around the corner of the prison to the captain's office.

A hundred convicts who were not part of the escaping crowd had rushed to the scene of the disorder and were themselves a yelling mob, ready no doubt, to make a rush for liberty themselves if they found the way clear. It was a moment for action—for a man with an eye and a voice to command—and Director Wilkins, a modest interior journalist, proved that man.

Whipping out his revolver, Wilkins pointed it at the crowd of excited convicts, stepping back as he did so to make his position the more secure. Then he stopped, and in stern tones commanded them to enter the prison.

The door was unlocked for them and soon the bolt was shot with every man of the crowd on the inside. Wilkins did not mention the incident to anybody afterward, and even many of the officers were not made aware of the manner in which the director saved a possible general rush from the prison.[108]

The same day the report was submitted, Red Gordon was reported captured in Texas. This was never confirmed.

October 16, 1903

Exactly one month after the report recommended pardons, three inmates who had assisted in either helping injured guards or trying to slow the escape were rewarded.

Several Convicts Pardoned by Pardee

Governor Rewards Men Who Assisted the Guards on the Occasion of the Jail Break at Folsom
Five Men Will Be Liberated on Monday and It Will Go Hard with Them If They Ever Get into Trouble Again and Are Sent Back to Prison

Sacramento, Oct. 16.—Governor Pardee tonight pardoned Convicts J. Casey and J. Martinez out of Folsom prison. He also commuted the sentences of O.P. Clark, Charles Abbott and W. Grider. The men will be liberated on Monday. These men are thus rewarded for their conduct in assisting the guards to prevent further escapes at the time when the thirteen convicts recently broke jail at Folsom. In connection with the commutation of sentences, it is understood that if either of the men is sent back to the state penitentiary for any further offense, he shall serve in addition to the sentence he may then receive the remainder of the sentence from which he is relieved at the present time.[109]

November 5, 1903

Sometime between August and November, Joseph Theron may have headed north from Carson City, as he was reported to have been captured in North Yakima, Washington.

> *If the descriptions given by prison authorities at Folsom Prison are not mixed, Fred Slocum who was arrested here last night by Sheriff Grant is Joseph Theron. He tallies exactly with the description of Theron, no 4113, who escaped from Folsom Prison, July 27 last.*
>
> *Theron was taken into custody in Bert Fletcher's saloon. He had been under surveillance all evening. He told Sheriff Grant that this was the first time that he had ever been arrested. He was put in the sweatbox at midnight last night and then admitted that he had been in Folsom Prison. He said he was sent there in 1897 for burglary and was released just one week after the famous jail break, but he said his number was 4049 and that the descriptions of himself and Theron have been mixed. He says he has been arrested before for Theron. He told the Sheriff in detail how the escape of the prisoners was made but denies he was one of them.*[110]

However, if the *Marysville (CA) Daily Appeal* of November 8, 1903, is to be believed, it wasn't him but another man named Fred Slocum.

> *Fred Slocum, who was arrested at North Yakima, Wash., on suspicion that he was Joseph Theron, one of the escaped convicts from Folsom, is known by our police officers. Officer McCoy arrested Slocum in this city on the first last September (circus day). He was in company of an ex-convict named Welch, who was sent to Folsom from Sutter County. Both men were acting suspiciously, and after being locked up all night were ordered to leave town and went to Chico. Slocum is a two-termer and was discharged from Folsom on the 31st of last August. His picture is in the rogue's gallery at the police office. His description tallies in some respects with that of Theron.*

DECEMBER 1, 1903

Warden Wilkinson resigned and was replaced by Archibald Yell. The new warden had a different perspective on incarceration. Beyond taking command of Folsom Prison, Yell wanted it shut down, as he said the state of the prisons as well as their geography made them ill-suited to successful rehabilitation, which he declared an "absolute and utter impossibility."

The appointment of Yell was a surprise to some, as J.M. Stanley, the former sheriff of Mendocino County, had been cited in some reports as being a favorite for replacement.[111]

It wasn't just that Yell wanted to repair old walls and build new ones—he wanted the prisoners off the mainland.

> *He suggested prisons constructed off the coast of California on islands with sufficient water, farmland, and building-stone. In addition to preventing escapes like the one in July 1903, the islands would provide proximity to coastal merchants, who would purchase commodities produced with prison labor. Moreover, the prison could purchase supplies for cheaper than by rail, and the island-prisons would have access to fuel from oil wells off the shore of California.*[112]

Yell was lauded as having a "strong hand [that] grasped the complicated details of prison industries." The *Mountain Democrat* continued, "In his appointment, the directors made no mistake, and it all means that subject to their rightful supervision, Folsom Prison and prisoners have a commander-in-chief, who knows his powers, and will not hesitate to perform them."

The lack of hesitation to perform his duties may be referring to the order made around the same time to finally build a wall, after pressure from many sides, including the California state legislature, which wrote the escape "may also be attributed to lack of a properly executed building plan, since such an emeute would have small chance for success in a well-walled and well-arranged prison."[113]

The decision to build the wall finally came from the California state prison directors, who bravely voted unanimously to build a wall around Folsom Prison that was much like the walls built years earlier at San Quentin with the belief that perhaps if there had been a wall the Big Break wouldn't have happened. With all of the haste surrounding the new wall, construction didn't start until 1909 and wasn't completed until 1923, twenty years after the escape.

While he did not close down Folsom and build prisons in the Pacific off California, Yell did make changes, including reversing several decisions related to personnel that had been made by his predecessor. Among them was restoring George Lamphrey as turnkey.[114] He had been dismissed due to rumors that he was after Wilkinson's job or because he had earned the enmity of inmates.

Yell served as warden at Folsom until 1909, when he was replaced by J.J. Smith. Conjecture at the time was that his removal as warden may have been caused by Yell being ahead of his time with a focus on rehabilitation, rather than punishment, or it may have been constant haranguing of state legislators who did not buy into his vision.

FEBRUARY 24, 1904

Not long after leaving Folsom, former warden Thomas Wilkinson died in Oakland, California.

"Thomas Wilkinson Dead—Former Warden of Folsom Prison Passes Away in Oakland," read the headline, followed by, "Ex-Warden Thomas Wilkinson of Folsom prison died this morning at his residence in East Oakland. The deceased was in charge of the penitentiary at the time of the big outbreak. He was seized by the escaping convicts and compelled to walk along with them, acting as a shield to prevent the guards from shooting. They kept him in custody until they had fled a couple of miles from prison. He was then relieved of most of his clothing and allowed to go. Shortly afterward Wilkinson was succeeded in the wardenship by Archibald Yell, who is now the incumbent."[115]

FEBRUARY 26, 1904

Ed Waters, Harry Gibbs and G.N. Hair, who were working on the train from Newcastle to Auburn where Albert Seavis was discovered, were awarded $550 by the California State Board of Examiners for their role in his capture.

According to contemporary reports, Sheriff Keena did not claim a portion of the reward.

Waters, Gibbs and Hair, while likely appreciative of the reward, may have had no idea how lucky they were to receive it. While it may have been founded on the promise of gold, California's government was notably tightfisted with sharing its good fortune, especially related to claims for payment. Joseph Silvera submitted a letter to the State Board of Prison Directors[116] with a request for $700 reimbursement for horses killed by posses and accompanying prison guards during the Battle of Pilot Hill, but he was rebuked with a comment in the *San Francisco Call*: "The directors thought that a thousand more bills of the same kind might appear and that it would be better not to establish a bad precedent by the payment of the first."

August 26, 1903

A seamstress and her assistant at 909 Clay Street in San Francisco were robbed by two men with guns, who, after threatening the two women, left with silver and jewelry. San Francisco police attributed the crime to Ray Fahey and Fred Howard, whom they believe were in the city. This brazen robbery was only one of several, including several saloon robberies they believed this pair were responsible for. Reports also stated Ed Davis was thought to be with Fahey and Howard.

This followed Fahey and Davis reportedly being spotted by detectives in the Sacramento train station, attempting to board a freight train bound for San Francisco.

After the reported robberies, Davis and Howard were not seen in California for many years. Perhaps they made enough to make their way east.

January 26, 1911

The 1903 escape from Folsom Prison wasn't the only one from this prison or others in California that may have been driven by extreme punishment and torture of prisoners. After years of complaints, progress on prisoner rights began to be made, and on January 26, 1911, the Assembly of the State Legislature of California instructed the Committee on State Prisons and Reformatories to investigate "to what extent, punishment is used in the state prisons of California, and especially to what extent the strait-jacket is used therein."

September 1, 1941

By the time former governor George Pardee died at age eighty-four in his hometown of Oakland, California, in September 1941, he had been out of office for more than thirty years. His time after he left office in Sacramento had been busy, as he had returned to practicing medicine, helped found the California chapter of the Bull Moose Party and drove the creation of the East Bay Municipal Utility District, which he helped lead for many years.

His death came just a few months before the opening of the California Institute for Men (CIM) in Chino, the first state prison for men to open since Folsom roughly sixty years before. Chino was the apex of a period of exploration of rehabilitation over punishment and the separation of the different types of criminals that Pardee had called for in his inaugural address.

A report written in 2011 described the opening and attitude toward prisoners: "This prison environment, so different from today, came about in the late-1930s when the Legislature decided to segregate the hardened criminals from those 'capable of moral rehabilitation and restoration to good citizenship.'"

The first warden at Chino—who disdained that title and preferred to be called a supervisor—believed in rehabilitation first and punishment as a last resort.

He believed that many first-time wrong doers could be turned into productive citizens by not being mixed in with hard-core criminals at San Quentin and Folsom.

"A prison experience is too apt to bring out the worst in a man and leave its permanent scar upon his personality," he wrote in "Prisoners Are People," his 1951 book about the Chino experience."[117]

By the 1970s and 1980s, however, times began to change, and politicians passed more "tough-on-crime" legislation, putting many more people behind bars, and jamming prisons. CIM, which had 1,474 prisoners in 1944, had 6,229 in 1991 and about 6,600 at its height several years ago.

Overcrowding, and the growth of gangs in and out of prison, have resulted in guards armed with guns and rifles, manned guard towers and a more traditional prison environment.

Nearly one hundred years later, there are still the same concerns about prisons, prisoners and crime, and every time there are steps forward on improving conditions and outcomes, there are steps backward toward punishment and torture.

Some Stories Never End

Thirteen prisoners escaped Folsom Prison on July 27, 1903. More than one hundred years later, we know how many of their stories ended, but not all.

Of the thirteen who escaped that day, there were many different paths. One died at his own hand on the run, two at the end of a rope back in Folsom Prison.

J.J. Allison died from gunshot wounds, both from pursuers and self-inflicted, in the back of a wagon on a road in Pilot Hill on the day of the escape.

Albert Seavis was recaptured in Auburn, California, on August 3, 1903. He was discharged from Folsom Prison on parole in 1924.

Joseph Murphy was captured in Reno just eight days after the escape. He was found guilty of the murder of Guard William Cotter during the escape. He was executed by hanging at Folsom Prison on July 14, 1905.

James P. Roberts was captured in Davisville nine days after the break and stayed in Folsom Prison until he was paroled in 1913, ten years and three months after his escape.

John Wood was recaptured in Reno, Nevada, while getting a shave and a haircut in a barbershop. He died by suicide, hanging, after capture and being convicted of murdering the two militiamen who were killed as they charged up Manzanita Hill.

FRED HOWARD was caught in Colorado in 1908 and transferred to San Quentin Prison in California, where he stayed until returning to Folsom Prison in 1923, twenty years after his escape. He died in Folsom Prison in 1941.

EDWARD DAVIS, who slammed a book closed, giving the signal for the escape to start, was captured in North Dakota in 1911, where he was living under the alias Bill Miner. It wasn't luck that he was recaptured. He was the subject of another manhunt after being suspected of the abduction of a local woman. There is no record of his being returned to California to complete his prison term.

HARRY ELDRIDGE was captured near Seattle in 1904. He was tried and convicted of the murder of Guard William Cotter. He was executed by hanging at Folsom Prison.

OF THE FIVE WHO weren't captured, Theron and Miller were in the Manzanita Gang and likely continued east past Reno, and Gordon, Case and Fahey were part of the Sacramento Gang. According to reports, they continued west to San Francisco and beyond.

FRANK CASE was last seen headed toward Sacramento after the Battle of Pilot Hill. He was never recaptured, and his final whereabouts are unknown.

RAY FAHEY was reported as possibly stealing a horse near Sacramento and then suspected of several other crimes in San Francisco in late August 1903. He was never recaptured, and his whereabouts are unknown.

JOSEPH THERON was last seen when he poked his head into a barbershop outside Reno while John Wood was getting a shave and a haircut right before he was captured. He was never recaptured, and his whereabouts are unknown.

FRANK MILLER was last seen on August 14, 1903, running away from deputies in Reno, Nevada. Some reports say he went underwater in the Truckee River during this secondary escape and never came up. He was never recaptured, and his whereabouts are unknown.

RICHARD M. "RED" GORDON was last seen heading toward Sacramento after the Battle of Pilot Hill. There was a report of his being captured in Jacksonville, Texas, in September 1903. There were also reports from Missouri of his demise and even some whispers that he was killed by Murphy and Eldridge and his body dumped in an abandoned mine shaft near Dutch Flat, thirty miles east of Pilot Hill. None of the reports of his capture or death was substantiated or confirmed. Whether he was recaptured or not was never confirmed. He was never returned to California, and his whereabouts are unknown.

AFTERWORD

Less than fifty-five years passed from the time of the gold discovery at Sutter's Mill to the big breakout at Folsom Prison. In this time, California's non-Native population had grown from approximately 20,000 in 1848 to 1.7 million by 1903. From the day at Sutter's Mill to building mines that transformed the environment, to the rise of cities from Sacramento to San Francisco to Los Angeles—and the crime that came with that incredible growth—the transformation of California from remote outpost to one of the largest economies in the world was well underway.

With the escape happening in the early years of the twentieth century, it's important to remember that this area in many ways was still the Wild West of old. Outside the major cities, law enforcement was often up to individuals, and when sheriffs needed assistance, they had to bring together a posse of locals to ride out on horses after their quarry.

In 1903, California was still early in its European-influenced history and finding its way with how to balance public safety and law and order with the freewheeling openness that had brought many west. This came with a need to direct necessary spending on incarceration, with the public wanting to spend the tax revenue on other—in their eyes—more productive means. The clashes between the prison directors and the legislators and the prisoners and the wardens and guards made this clear, with each side saying not enough and too much was being done.

After being recaptured, Fred Howard spent the rest of his life at Folsom Prison and was described as being "an old man who sits in the shade of the engine shed, at the head of the tramway—and with his single eye—gazes out across the valley to the green hills beyond the river."[118] He wouldn't talk about the escape of 1903 unless asked, and "when the name of Red Shirt Gordon is mentioned, the droop of the shoulder noticeably lessens, the eye loses its lacklustre appearance, and he speaks haltingly—as though careful of his choice of words—of 'The Leader.' He doesn't believe the stories of Red being caught, or killed, or in jail, he believes he's still out there and still 'beating the law.'"[119]

AUTHOR'S CONNECTION

In the introduction for this book, I mentioned a letter received by Etta Steinman from (we believe) Albert Wilkinson, the son of Thomas Wilkinson, warden of Folsom Prison. Etta Steinman was my great-grandmother. She grew up in Sacramento with a front-row seat during a time of incredible growth. Her father was a leading businessman who worked for Leland Stanford and served on the city council and as mayor.

The letter that started the story:

My dear Miss Steinman,

Your welcome letter came to hand on the 12th.

We were so very glad to know that you are all well and having an enjoyable time and we appreciate your kind thoughts and sympathy. No one except they who have been through a similar experience can ever realize the horror of that morning—When [name] came and told me that they had my father and Captain Murphy in the Captain's office and were cutting them to pieces with knives. You can imagine my terror.

I hurried in my clothing and ran to Mr. Wilkin's room. (He and two friends had remained over from the board meeting). He had heard the reports and was dressing as fast as he could. I assured Miss [Newman] then went downstairs where the second report came that the convicts had taken them off with them. It was some time before I learned that they also had Harold. I was relieved when I found they had taken them away for I knew they were alive.

Then pandemonium began in the prison. The convicts howled, yelled, shrieked, whistled, and pounded on the windows. We were told to leave the house as they would break through and in case they did the Gatling guns would be turned on and we would not be safe—so went through the garden to the valley to my nephew's house—when we got to the top of the hill a guard told us my father had just come back and gone into the prison and all at once all was as still as a grave inside—Well!

Can you imagine my terror for I thought they were tearing him to pieces, and I expected to see him come out in sections. Instead, they crowded around him, and congratulated him on his safety and narrow escape. He ordered them to go to their cells and strange to say they went, most of them willingly but some of the villains hung back but he said, "Go to your cells at once!" and they

Original letter to author's great-grandmother from Albert Wilkinson, son of the warden of Folsom Prison in 1903 (p. 1). *Courtesy of author.*

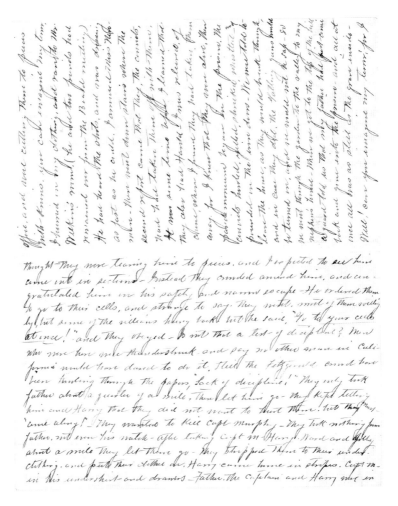

Original letter to author's great-grandmother from Albert Wilkinson, son of the warden of Folsom Prison in 1903 (p. 2). *Courtesy of author.*

obeyed. Isn't that a lot of discipline? Men were now more than thunderstruck and say no other man in California would have dared to do it.

They only took father about a quarter of a mile then let him go. They kept telling him and Harry that they did not want to hurt them, but they must come along. They wanted to kill Capt. Murphy. They took nothing from father, not even his watch. After taking Capt. M, Harry, Ward, and J about a mile they let them go. They stripped them to their underclothing and put their clothes on. Harry came home in stripes. Capt. M in his undershirt and drawers.

Father, the captain and Harry were in the captain's office when the convicts made a rush for them. The first one came charging in and struck at Harry with a knife. A fine thing Harry dodged the knife went through his hat. Then he struck out and kicked the convict clean out of the office in his shock. He was so dazed that he did not get away—when they went for father + Capt. Cochrane came to his assistance, and they cut him awfully and poor Cotter they disemboweled. [Then] *more than two or three convicts to an official, and they had had such murderous looking knives and they came to* <u>kill</u> *them all, unless the gates are opened. If father had* [been alone] *he would have ordered the Gatling guns fired for he cares nothing for life, but he could not take the responsibility of the lives of his men—they slashed father across the abdomen with a razor there was a wound a finger long not deep thank God! They slashed right through coat, vest, and shirts. Mr. Jack was cut in the side of the neck his collar saved him. It is strange so few of them have been caught.*

The sheriff's, newspaper reporters and militia are on the case, if they are not caught, we shall have some trouble here. I am sure you must be weary of reading—so I will say no more on this subject.

Notwithstanding all this trouble we are well. The summer has been delightfully cool and if this had not occurred, we would have passed a very pleasant summer. The parrots are well and seem quite happy and content although they call for "Etta" and "Ben" every day. I hope you will have a pleasant time and will return feeling well paid for your trip.

My father joins me in kindest messages to you. I have received your postals and thank you much for remembering me.

With love I will close with Auf wiedersehen. Antoinette will be much pleased to hear from you again, A

NOTES

Introduction

1. Black, *You Can't Win*, 360.

Chapter 1

2. *San Francisco Call*, September 17, 1903.

Chapter 2

3. Upton, *Pioneers of El Dorado*, 6–7.
4. Ibid., 8.

Chapter 3

5. Soule, Gihon and Nisbet, *Annals of San Francisco*, 230.
6. Ibid., 233.
7. FoundSF, "Prison Ship 'Euphemia,'" www.foundsf.org.
8. Ruesch, *Excepts from Langley Porter Institute*.
9. Delgado and Frank, "Gold Rush Enterprise," 321–30.

10. McKanna, "1851–1880," 50; Historic American Buildings Survey, San Quentin State Prison Building 22, National Park Service, www.loc.gov.

11. Secrest, *Behind San Quentin's Walls*, 26.

12. Winfrey, "California Prison's Maritime History."

13. Nephew, "History of Folsom Prison," 2.

14. Starr, *California*, 109.

15. Journal of the House, 1859.

16. Black, *You Can't Win*, 272.

17. California Department of Corrections, "1857."

18. Nephew, "History of Folsom Prison," 3.

19. Forty-five inmates, per Nephew, "History of Folsom Prison"; forty-four, per Brown, *Folsom Prison*.

20. Gold Country Media, "Folsom A to Z," https://goldcountrymedia.com.

21. Brown, *130 Years*, 3.

22. Nephew, "History of Folsom Prison," 20.

23. *San Francisco Call*, June 29, 1899.

24. *Los Angeles Herald*, November 12, 1899.

25. California Department of Corrections and Rehabilitation, "Folsom Warden Aull Was Longtime Lawman, Part 2," *Unlocking History*, October 10 2019, www.cdcr.ca.gov.

26. Folsom Prison Appointment Certificate, California State Archives F3717:1303 Corrections Folsom Prison Appointment certificate 1899.

27. *San Francisco Call*, May 22, 1902.

28. Ibid.

29. *San Francisco Call*, July 16, 1902.

30. Ibid.

31. The Governors' Gallery, "George Pardee, Inaugural Address," https://governors.library.ca.gov/addresses/21-Pardee.html.

32. *San Francisco Call*, February 15, 1903.

Chapter 4

33. Gold Country Media, "Folsom A to Z."

34. Nephew, "History of Folsom Prison," 18.

35. "They Dug for Liberty," *Deseret Weekly*, October 4, 1890.

36. Ibid.

37. Sontag and Warner, *Pardoned Lifer*.

Chapter 5

38. *Los Angeles Times*, September 10, 2000.

Chapter 6

39. *Sacramento Union*, November 18, 1897.
40. *San Francisco Call*, June 18, 1898.
41. Ibid.
42. "Back to Prison," *San Jose Herald*, August 7, 1900.
43. *Weekly Independent* (Elko, NV), August 10, 1900.
44. *San Francisco Call*, February 10, 1900.
45. *Appendix to the Journals of the Senate*.
46. *San Francisco Call*, July 24, 1901.
47. *San Francisco Call*, January 25, 1902.
48. *San Francisco Call*, November 4, 1901.
49. *Los Angeles Herald*, February 5, 1902.
50. Bates, *History of the Bench and Bar*.
51. Carey, *By the Golden Gate*.
52. San Francisco Call, February 14, 1902.
53. "Safe Crackers Were Baffled," *Stockton Record*, December 12, 1902.
54. *Contra Costa Gazette*, February 28, 1903.
55. "Harry Eldridge Again Convicted," *San Francisco Chronicle*, March 25, 1903.
56. *Oakland Tribune*, February 7, 1963.
57. *San Francisco Call*, March 31, 1903.
58. *Past and Present of Alameda County*.
59. *San Francisco Call*, January 31, 1903.

Chapter 7

60. Report of the State Prison Board of Directors, September 16, 1903.
61. Folsom Historical Society, "Break of 1903."
62. Black, *You Can't Win*, 270.
63. *California Historian*, Fall 1998.
64. Report of the State Board of Prison Directors, September 16, 1903
65. Ibid.
66. Folsom Historical Society, "Break of 1903."

67. Willis, *History of Sacramento County*, 277.
68. *Los Angeles Herald*, July 30, 1903.
69. *San Francisco Call*, July 28, 1903.
70. Moore, *Folsom's 93*.

Chapter 8

71. *Daily Morning Union*, July 30, 1903.
72. *Daily Morning Union*, July 29, 1903.
73. *Los Angeles Herald*, July 30, 1903.

Chapter 9

74. *State of California v. John H. Woods*.
75. *California v. John H. Wood and Joseph Murphy*.
76. *California v. John H. Wood*.

Chapter 10

77. Peabody, "How About That!" 86.
78. California Native Plant Society, "Common Manzanita," https://calscape.org.
79. *Wide World Magazine*, 36.
80. State of California, JB Lauck Adjutant General, State of California, Courtesy California State Archives.
81. *Daily Morning Union*, August 4, 1903.
82. *Mountain Democrat*, August 8, 1903.
83. *Daily Morning Union*, August 9, 1903.
84. Ibid.

Chapter 11

85. County of El Dorado Cemetery Administration, "Placerville Union," https://www.edcgov.us.
86. *Daily Morning Union*, August 6, 1903.
87. Harpster, *Genesis of Reno*.

Chapter 12

88. Localwiki, "Putah Creek," Davis, https://localwiki.org.
89. *San Francisco Call*, August 6, 1903.
90. *Daily Morning Union*, August 8, 1903.
91. American Presidency Project, "Theodore Roosevelt Remarks at Colfax, California," www.presidency.ucsb.edu.
92. Lardner and Brock, *History of Placer and Nevada Counties*.
93. *Colusa Daily Sun*, August 7, 1903.
94. *San Francisco Call*, August 7, 1903.
95. *Wide World Magazine*.
96. *Merced County Sun*, August 1, 1913.
97. *Journals of the Legislature*.
98. *Nevada State Journal*, September 19, 1903.

Chapter 13

99. *Evening Bee*, July 14, 1905.
100. *Hanford Journal*, July 18, 1905.
101. John, "Brutal 'Oregon Boot.'"
102. Information taken from Folsom Prison prisoner photo.
103. *San Francisco Call*, September 17, 1911.
104. Letter from Judge E.C. Hart to JT Bevan, Clerk, State Board of Prison Directors, Represa, CA September 3, 1911.
105. Letter from Eugene S. Wachhorst, District Attorney, Sacramento County, California, November 18, 1911.
106. Smokey's Last Farewell.

Epilogue

107. Brown, *History of Folsom*.
108. *Grass Valley and Nevada City Daily Morning Union*, July 30, 1903.
109. *Press Democrat*, October 17, 1903.
110. *San Francisco Call*, November 7, 1903.
111. *Riverside Enterprise*, November 14, 1903.
112. Beard, "Review of an Environmental History of Incarceration."
113. *Journals of the Legislature*.

114. *San Francisco Call*, July 3, 1904.
115. *Press Democrat*, February 25, 1904.
116. Moore, *Folsom's 93*.
117. *Inland Valley Daily Bulletin*, March 14, 2011.

Afterword

118. Folsom Historical Society, "Break of 1903."
119. Ibid.

BIBLIOGRAPHY

American Presidency Project. "Remarks at Colfax, California." www. presidency.ucsb.edu.

Appendix to the Journals of the Senate and Assembly of California 35, no. 1.

Bates, Joseph Clement. *History of the Bench and Bar of California*. San Francisco: Bench and Bar Publishing, 1912.

Beard, Augustine. "Review of an Environmental History of Incarceration in California, 1851–1990." Thesis, University of Oregon, 2018.

Black, Jack. *You Can't Win*. New York: Simon and Schuster, 2013.

Brown, Jim. *Folsom Prison*. Images of America. Charleston, SC: Arcadia Publishing, 2008.

———. *130 Years of the Folsom Prison Legend*. Sacramento, CA: Capital Graphics, 2010.

Brown, Michael D. *History of Folsom Prison, 1878–1978*. Folsom, CA: Folsom Graphic Arts, [1978?].

California Department of Corrections. "1857: Records Shed Light on Early San Quentin." CDCR Time Capsule. November 14, 2019. https://www. cdcr.ca.gov.

California Native Plant Society. "Calscape—Restore Nature One Garden at a Time." https://calscape.org.

Carey, Joseph. *By the Golden Gate*. Albany, NY: Albany Diocesan Press, 1902.

Chaddock, Don, ed. "1857: Records Shed Light on Early San Quentin." Inside CDCR. November 14, 2019. https://www.cdcr.ca.gov.

Delgado, James P., and Russell Frank. "A Gold Rush Enterprise: Sam Ward, Charles Mersch, and the Storeship *Niantic*." *Huntington Library Quarterly* 6, no. 4 (Autumn 1983): 321–30.

El Dorado County. "Placerville Union." Cemetery Administration. https://www.edcgov.us.

Folsom Historical Society. "Break of 1903." Monograph.

Harpster, Jack. *The Genesis of Reno*. Reno: University of Nevada Press, 2016.

John, Finn J.D. "Brutal 'Oregon Boot' Made Our State Prison Infamous." *Offbeat Oregon*, March 9, 2014. https://offbeatoregon.com

Journal of the House of Assembly of California, at the tenth session of the legislature, 1859.

Journals of the Legislature of the State of California 1 (1905).

Lardner, William Branson, and Michael John Brock. *History of Placer and Nevada Counties, California*. Los Angeles, CA: Historic Record Co., 1924.

McKanna, Clare V. "1851–1880: The Origins of San Quentin." *California History*, March 1987.

Moore, April. *Folsom's 93: The Lives and Crimes of Folsom Prison's Executed Men*. Fresno, CA: Linden Publishing, 2013.

Nephew, David A. "The History of Folsom Prison and Its Disciplinary Policies, 1856–1903" *Golden Notes* 39, Nos. 3, 4 (Fall and Winter 1993).

Past and Present of Alameda County, California. Vol. 2. Chicago: S.J. Clarke Publishing Company, 1914.

Peabody, George. "How About That!" *El Dorado County CA Historical Anthology*, 1989.

Report of the State Board of Prison Directors of California on Recent Outbreak at Folsom Prison, Dated September 16, 1903.

Review of *State of California v. John H. Wood*. 1905. Supreme Court of California.

Ruesch, Jurgen, MD. *Excerpts from Langley Porter Institute and Psychiatry in Northern California: 1943–1975*. San Francisco, CA: Friends of Langley Porter Institute, 1978.

Secrest, William B. *Behind San Quentin's Walls*. Fresno, CA: Craven Street Books, 2015.

Smokey's Last Farewell. Letter from California State Archives. Sacramento, CA.

Sontag, George, and Opie L. Warner. *A Pardoned Lifer*. San Bernardino, CA: Index Print, 1909.

Soule, Frank, John H. Gihon and James Nisbet. *Annals of San Francisco*. Berkeley, CA: Berkeley Hills Books, 1999.

Starr, Kevin. *California: A History*. New York: Modern Library, 2005.

State of California, JB Lauck, Adjutant General, State of California, Courtesy California State Archives.

Thompson, Don. "Grim Exhibits Reveal Why Inmates Had Those Folsom Prison Blues." *Los Angeles Times*, September 10, 2000.

Upton, Charles Elmer. *Pioneers of El Dorado*. Placerville, CA: C.E. Upton, 1906.

Wide World Magazine, April 1904.

Willis, William Ladd. *History of Sacramento County, California*. Los Angeles, CA: Historic Record Co., 1913.

Winfrey, Tommy. "A California Prison's Maritime History." *San Quentin News*, March 13, 2013. http://sanquentinnews.com.

ABOUT THE AUTHOR

J osh Morgan lives in the Sierra Nevada foothills of California with his wife and two daughters. You'll often find him running trails through the gold country and exploring Northern California, where his family has lived since the 1860s. Josh earned undergraduate and graduate degrees from the University of the Pacific and works at Sierra College.

Visit us at
www.historypress.com